tackl BULLYING in your school

This book provides teachers and other educational professionals with an accessible, yet comprehensive and detailed guide to tackling bullying in schools. It gives essential facts and figures about the problem of bullying behaviour and then offers step-by-step descriptions of strategies and activities for dealing with it. The book discusses:

- how to establish a whole school anti-bullying policy
- curriculum-based intervention strategies
- methods for responding directly to bullying situations
- techniques for tackling bullying during breaks and lunchtimes

The book is unique in drawing together the broad spectrum of types of intervention strategy and describing them in sufficient detail for teachers to put them into practice immediately. Each section has been written by an acknowledged expert on the field and all of the intervention strategies have been tried and tested by teachers in both primary and secondary schools.

Sonia Sharp works for Barnsley LEA as an Educational Psychologist. She has worked extensively with schools to establish successful anti-bullying strategies. **Peter Smith** is Professor of Psychology at the University of Sheffield and has published widely, including *The Psychology of Grandparenthood* (Routledge), *Play in Animals and Humans* and *Practical Approaches to Bullying*.

tackling BULLYING in your school

A PRACTICAL
HANDBOOK
FOR TEACHERS

edited by

SONIA SHARP

and

PETER K. SMITH

LONDON AND NEW YORK

First published 1994
by Routledge

11 New Fetter Lane, London EC4P 4EE
Simultaneously published in the USA and Canada
by Routledge
29 West 35th Street, New York, NY 10001

©1994 Sonia Sharp and Peter K. Smith

Typeset in Palatino by Florencetype Ltd, Kewstoke, Avon

Printed and bound in Great Britain by
Clays Ltd, St. Ives PLC

British Library Cataloguing in Publication Data

A catalogue record for this book is available from
the British Library

Library of Congress Cataloging in Publication Data

Tackling bullying in your school:
a practical handbook for teachers
edited by Sonia Sharp and Peter K. Smith.
p. cm.
Includes biographical references to (p.   ).
1. Bullying.
2. School psychology.
I. Smith, Peter K.
II. Sharp, Sonia, 1961–
BF637. B85T33   1994   93–47626 CIP
371.5'8—dc20
ISBN 0-415-10374-6

contents

illustrations

Tables

Figures

contributors

Tiny Arora is Specialist Senior Psychologist for North Yorkshire LEA and Honorary Lecturer, Division of Education, Sheffield University.

Mike Boulton is a Lecturer in the Department of Psychology, University of Keele.

Helen Cowie is Director of Counselling Studies and Reader in Social Studies at Bretton Hall College (College of the University of Leeds) Nr Wakefield.

Catherine Higgins is a Lecturer in the Landscape Department, University of Sheffield.

Sonia Sharp is an Educational Psychologist for Barnsley LEA.

Peter K. Smith is Professor of Psychology in the Department of Psychology, Sheffield University.

David Thompson is Director of the MSc in Educational Psychology, Division of Education, Sheffield University.

Irene Whitney is a Research Assistant, Leicester University.

acknowledgements

Most of us would agree that bullying is not something we want in our schools. However, it is something which all schools have some experience of. We hope that this book will offer schools everywhere some ideas and strategies for tackling the problem of bullying behaviour. We also hope that as a result of action against bullying, schools everywhere will become places where all pupils feel safer and happier.

Many of the ideas presented in this handbook are not new, although for some of them this is the first time they have been applied specifically to bullying behaviour. We would like to thank all of the schools, in Sheffield and elsewhere, which have helped us by trying out different activities and strategies and, most importantly, have let us know how successfully (or otherwise) they have been implemented. We would also like to thank the 'experts', not only in the UK but also abroad, who have helped us to build up a repertoire of successful strategies. Thanks must go to the funding bodies who have enabled some of the research into the problem of bullying and evaluation of different strategies. These are the Department for Education which made possible the DFE Sheffield Anti-Bullying Project; the Calouste Gulbenkian Foundation, which has not only financially supported a number of initiatives but also continually encouraged work against bullying; the ESRC for enabling important studies into the nature of bullying, in particular for those pupils with special educational needs.

Additional thanks go to Sarah Barron, upon whose superb organisational skills this work has depended; to Martin Gazzard and Don Pennock for guiding us and establishing important links within the LEA; to Ed Jones for being prepared to word-process diagrams at the last moment.

about this handbook . . .

This handbook aims to provide you with a range of practical strategies for tackling bullying in your school. The ideas and approaches described in the book are based on the work of individual practitioners, acknowledged experts and research projects both in the UK and abroad. All of them have been tried and tested in UK schools and are accepted as workable within a school environment. No individual intervention is always going to be 100 per cent successful; we therefore recommend that you use the ideas in this book to develop a *range* of ways for preventing and responding to bullying behaviour in your school.

The first chapter of the book aims to provide you with important *information about the nature of bullying behaviour* generally. When tackling bullying, you and your colleagues should be well informed about the problem and common myths and stereotypes about bullying behaviour should be challenged. The second chapter describes *survey techniques* to help you find out how much bullying is going on in your school. Obtaining an individual school profile of bullying behaviour is an essential first step in intervention. This can assist with motivating staff to take action; targeting specific interventions and monitoring changes in bullying behaviour over time. This section offers guidelines for designing your own survey; advice on where you can find 'ready-made' surveys and examples of questionnaires for you to use.

In the third chapter, attention is focused on *establishing a whole-school policy* against bullying. This is a core intervention. Any school which is considering taking action against bullying should begin by establishing an anti-bullying policy. This kind of policy should provide a framework for implementing any other kinds of intervention. A model for policy development is provided.

Each of the subsequent chapters describes interventions aimed at a particular sector of the school community. Chapter 4 considers the *curriculum* as a vehicle for involving all pupils in addressing the issue of bullying. It demonstrates how pupils can be encouraged to be more careful of their own behaviour and take action when they encounter other pupils being bullied. The activities described in this section are intended to be awareness-raising and preventative.

Chapter 5 introduces particular *strategies for responding to bullying situations*. It focuses on a Swedish method for counselling pupils who bully others and a set of assertive strategies which can be taught to pupils who regularly experience bullying from their peers. These interventions target those pupils directly involved in bullying situations and aim to support the pupils in finding their own solutions to their interpersonal difficulties.

In Chapters 6 and 7, the *playground* becomes the focus of attention. These two sections are aimed particularly at the primary school but secondary schools may also find them helpful. Whether primary or secondary, school breaks and lunchtimes can be hazardous times for bullied pupils. Boredom, poor supervision and an unfriendly environment can all encourage bullying behaviour. In Chapter 6, the difficulties faced by supervisors and how schools can enhance the quality of supervision are considered. In Chapter 7, a model for improving the school grounds in ways which will encourage co-operative behaviour is offered.

Chapter 8 provides a brief overview of *resources* available to schools. From this section you will be able to find sources of information, videos and literature which can help you in implementing your interventions against bullying. The resource section is divided into subsections relating to other sections of this book.

Collectively, the sections offer a comprehensive anti-bullying approach for any school. Thoroughness is important in creating a social climate which rejects bullying behaviour and promotes co-operative behaviour. We strongly recommend that schools attempt to intervene at all of the levels described in the individual chapters of this book: by developing a whole-school policy; by encouraging collective responsibility for the problem through the curriculum; by improving the environment beyond the classroom – the corridors, the school grounds, the toilets; by responding quickly and effectively to bullying situations which arise and by supporting those pupils who are directly involved.

All of the authors who have contributed to this book have been involved in the DFE-funded Sheffield Anti-Bullying Project, as well as other initiatives relating to tackling bullying behaviour in schools. The DFE Sheffield Anti-Bullying Project was funded by the government to identify effective strategies for reducing levels of bullying in schools. This project found that schools *can and do* make a difference to bullying behaviour and that successful schools used many of the ideas described in this book. One outcome of the project is a package written for schools offering an account of the project and advice based upon its findings. This package will have been made available to all schools in England and Wales.

Although we know that *all* schools have some bullying, each school is different and you will need to consider each of the interventions described here in relation to the individual nature of your school. You may find you need to adapt some of the activities to suit the needs of your pupils or your school.

What can you expect to achieve?

By thoroughly implementing the interventions described in this book, you can expect to achieve:

- a reduction in the number of pupils who report being bullied;
- a reduction in the duration of bullying incidents when they do arise;
- an increase in the number of pupils who report bullying behaviour;
- an increase in the number of pupils who would help if someone is being bullied;
- a majority of pupils (over 80 per cent) in the school who feel that your school does take action against bullying.

Do not underestimate the amount of time and effort you will need to commit in order to achieve these kinds of changes. Establishing an anti-bullying policy and implementing the different interventions in the first place can take at least one academic year. You may begin to see improvements straight away but sometimes it can take two or three years of continued and consistent implementation before you begin to see major changes throughout the school.

You are unlikely to eradicate bullying completely, but you can hope to significantly reduce the likelihood of bullying behaviour occurring and make sure it is responded to quickly and effectively when a bullying situation does occur. You can make your whole school environment safer and happier for all pupils and all staff.

There are broader benefits for schools who tackle bullying behaviour. General discipline is likely to be improved, relationships between staff and pupils can be enhanced. Parents are more confident in schools which take direct action against bullying.

What will you need?

There are some key ingredients for success in tackling bullying in schools. These are:

- a clear and unequivocal commitment from the headteacher and governing body to develop and implement an anti-bullying approach;
- a core group of interested individuals to co-ordinate the approach and to facilitate communication throughout the school community;
- access to sufficient time in staff and governor meetings to enable planning and discussion of the strategies;
- timetabling flexibility to enable involvement of pupils through the curriculum;
- willingness to involve parents in establishing interventions;
- time and energy to maintain efforts on a long-term basis.

You might find it helpful to enlist the support of people connected with your school. These may be other professionals who are directly involved with educational matters, such as educational psychologists or educational social workers, or they may be members of the local community, such as police officers, health visitors, local religious leaders.

O·N·E | understanding bullying

SONIA SHARP
PETER K. SMITH

Before you can begin to tackle the problem of bullying you need to make sure you and your colleagues fully understand the nature of the problem.

What is bullying?

Bullying is a form of aggressive behaviour which is usually hurtful and deliberate; it is often persistent, sometimes continuing for weeks, months or even years and it is difficult for those being bullied to defend themselves. Underlying most bullying behaviour is an abuse of power and a desire to intimidate and dominate.

Bullying takes many forms. It can be:

- *physical* – hitting, kicking, taking or damaging belongings;
- *verbal* – name-calling, insulting, repeated teasing, racist remarks;
- *indirect* – spreading nasty rumours; excluding someone from social groups.

Bullying behaviour can be very subtle. Once a pupil or group of pupils have established a bullying relationship with another pupil or group of pupils, they may only have to look threateningly to reinforce their fearfulness.

What are the effects of bullying behaviour?

Bullying behaviour can affect pupils in a number of ways. When pupils are bullied, their lives are made miserable. They may suffer injury. They may be unhappy about coming to school. Over time, they are likely to lose self-confidence and self-esteem, blaming themselves for 'inviting' the bullying behaviour. This unhappiness is likely to affect their concentration and learning. Some children may experience stress-related symptoms: stomach aches and headaches; nightmares or anxiety attacks. Some children will avoid being bullied by not going to school. Some children may even become afraid to leave the safety of their own home. In secondary schools, pupils may be making subject choices because they want to avoid particular individuals rather than being interested in or successful at that subject. In the long term, persistently bullied pupils are more likely to become depressed as adults. For a small number of pupils, bullying behaviour can actually endanger their lives, possibly leading to serious injury or even death.

If unchallenged, other pupils can learn that bullying is a quick and effective way of getting what they want. Bullying can pervade the relationships of pupils and become accepted as normal.

Pupils who are persistently involved in bullying others are much more likely as young adults to be convicted of anti-social behaviour offences. Unless challenged, they may continue to use bullying tactics in their relationships with other people.

How much bullying is there in schools?

In the UK, the most extensive survey of bullying behaviour so far was carried out in 1990 by Peter Smith and Irene Whitney, funded by the Calouste Gulbenkian Foundation. Using a questionnaire survey, they asked 2,623 primary pupils and 4,135 secondary pupils about their bullying experiences that term. This is what they found out:

TABLE 1.1   SURVEY OF BULLYING IN PRIMARY SCHOOLS

Primary Schools	More than once or twice a term (%)	At least once a week (%)
Number of pupils reporting being bullied	27	10
Number of pupils reporting bullying others	12	4

TABLE 1.2 SURVEY OF BULLYING IN SECONDARY SCHOOLS

Secondary Schools	More than once or twice a term (%)	At least once a week (%)
Number of pupils reporting being bullied	10	4
Number of pupils reporting bullying others	6	1

Source: I. Whitney and P.K. Smith, (1993) *Educational Research* 35, 3–25.

The levels of bullying behaviour varied from school to school but Whitney and Smith did not find any primary school with less than 19 per cent of its population reporting being bullied at some time during that term; and in secondary schools, no school had fewer than 8 per cent of pupils reporting this level of bullying. All schools have some bullying.

Name-calling, being physically hit and being threatened were the most frequent direct forms of bullying. Being isolated or deliberately left out of groups of class-mates, and having rumours spread about you, were common indirect ways of being bullied. As pupils become older, their experiences of being bullied become less frequent. There is usually a reduction of about 15 per cent per year. However, the severity of bullying does not decrease and those few pupils in year 11 who are being bullied are probably facing serious difficulties. Peak ages for taking part in bullying behaviour are 7 years and 13–14 years.

Where does it happen?

For most pupils, bullying occurs in and around school, the playground being the most common location. In primary schools, three-quarters of pupils who are bullied are bullied during the breaks or lunchtimes. In secondary schools, bullying is more evenly spread across school grounds, corridors and classrooms.

The small group of more persistently bullied pupils report that they are not only bullied in school but also on their way to and from school. For these pupils, some-times home is the only safe place.

Who is involved?

Everybody has the potential to be involved in bullying behaviour, either on the giving or receiving end. The most common perpetrators of bullying behaviour are individual boys or groups of several boys. Girls tend to bully in groups, often using indirect bullying which can be more difficult for teachers to detect. Boys are more likely to use more direct, physical forms of bullying.

It is usual for pupils involved in bullying to be in the same class or year group as the pupil they are bullying. You will probably find that there are some classes in your school where levels of bullying are unusually high. When there is an age difference, the bullying pupils tend to be older than their victims.

Children who are bullied at home or who see their parents or siblings bullying others may be more likely to bully in school. A child who regularly hears his or her parents discussing how they 'made somebody do something' or how they deliberately cheated or manipulated someone at work to achieve their aims may be encouraged to carry out similar tactics on his or her peers.

Most pupils will experience bullying in some form at some stage in their school lives, but some children may be more at risk of persistent bullying. Pupils who lack close friends in school and who are often alone or who find it difficult to be assertive with their peers are more likely to be bullied. Those pupils who are perceived as being 'different' from the majority of other pupils in some way can also be at risk. Some children may even provoke bullying behaviour by behaving inappropriately, for example, by barging in on games or being a nuisance.

Children with special educational needs are much more likely to be bullied than other pupils. This is especially so for pupils with moderate or mild learning difficulties.

Although there are some children who are more prone to being involved in bullying, you and your colleagues must be careful not to stereotype pupils. Some of the most charming and helpful pupils can be quite vicious to their peers; some of the most able and socially competent pupils can be experiencing regular bullying and be quite fearful of their tormentors.

Who do pupils tell?

Unless you take deliberate steps to talk with pupils about bullying and encourage them to tell you if they are being bullied, most pupils will only tell a friend or someone at home. A majority of secondary-aged pupils do not tell anyone that they have been bullied. Bullying behaviour is often deliberately hidden from teachers; bullied pupils may be reluctant to tell because they fear reprisal or because they feel that their experiences will not be taken seriously. Even if addressed directly by a teacher, a pupil may deny being bullied, preferring to 'put on a brave face'. When parents do find out about bullying, their children may beg them not to approach the school. This barrier of silence only helps to perpetuate the bullying.

How do pupils feel about bullying?

Most pupils do not like bullying behaviour and would like to be able to help their peers. For schools who want to do something about bullying, these pupils are important allies. Bullying behaviour is a part of the pupil culture and you will need to work participatively *with* your pupils to achieve change.

T·W·O

how to measure bullying in your school

SONIA SHARP
TINY ARORA
PETER K. SMITH
IRENE WHITNEY

Why you need to know

- To motivate staff and governors to take action against bullying.
- To raise awareness of the problem amongst staff, pupils and parents.
- To confirm exactly where bullying happens.
- To establish a baseline to measure against after you have intervened.

How can you measure bullying?

There are three ways of measuring bullying. These are:

- questionnaire-based surveys,
- interviews,
- individual pupil activities.

Questionnaire-based surveys

You can buy questionnaires which have been tried and tested to make sure they work well or you can make your own. Questionnaires are good for most pupils but they discriminate against pupils who find it difficult to read.

The survey service

Whole-school surveys are commercially available. One example of this is the Survey Service which has been run at Sheffield University. It uses the questionnaire developed by Dan Olweus in Norway, which has been adapted and used in schools for the DFE Sheffield Anti-Bullying Project. Schools receive the questionnaires and the instructions for administration and then return the completed questionnaires to the university for analysis. They receive a portfolio which provides a detailed account of the nature and extent of bullying in the school for the term leading up to the survey. This information is presented by class groups, year groups and gender. They are also told where in school bullying is occurring; whether pupils are likely to be telling someone about it; and how they feel about it.

From 1994, the Survey Service will not continue in this form; instead the survey materials will become available as a commercial package which will include the questionnaire and detailed guidelines for administration and scoring. You will be able to buy the package and carry out the survey for yourselves.

The questionnaire has been widely used both in the UK and overseas so you will be able to compare your own findings with others. For example, those figures quoted in Chapter 1 from the work of Whitney and Smith (1993) are based on this questionnaire.

Administration

This survey takes about 30 to 40 minutes to carry out. All pupils within the school should fill in the questionnaire on the same day. To increase anonymity, the administrator should be someone other than the pupils' usual teacher or form tutor. (For further information contact: Peter K. Smith, Department of Psychology, University of Sheffield, Sheffield S10 2TN.)

The 'Life in School' checklist

Another example is the 'Life in School' checklist, which enables levels of bullying to be identified for the preceding week. A copy of the checklist is included on page 19. This questionnaire was originally designed by Tiny Arora and has been updated by Wolverhampton LEA (1992).

INFORMATION BOX 2.1 MEASURING BULLYING WITH THE 'LIFE IN SCHOOL' CHECKLIST

About the checklist . . .

The checklist is a collection of things which might happen to a pupil in school during any one week. About half of these things are nice or neutral things and about half are more unpleasant. This mixture is deliberate. It draws attention away from bullying.

The checklist has three special features:

Flexibility the checklist exists in many different versions. The main variations are to do with wording, the inclusion of particular items or whether pupils are expected to put their names on it or not. You can change the checklist to meet the needs of your school. If you do change it, make sure you include an equal proportion of positive and negative items. If you wish to calculate 'The Bullying or General Aggression Index' you will need to keep in the six items which are mentioned in **Activity Box 2.1**.

An indirect but more precise measurement of bullying the checklist avoids the direct question 'Are you being bullied?' This question is avoided because:

- there are so many different kinds of bullying behaviour;
- children can define bullying in different ways;
- the word 'bullying' can be emotive and pupils may not answer honestly.

The checklist refers to the immediate past the pupil is only asked to report on those events which happened during the past week. Memories of events occurring more than one week ago can be inaccurate. For very young pupils, you may want to ask what happened to them the day before or even today (see **Information Box 2.2**).

What information can the checklist give?

The checklist provides the following information:

- a Bullying Index;
- a General Aggression Index;
- a comprehensive picture of 'Life in School';
- a means of identifying bullied pupils;
- any extra information you want (by putting your own questions in).

ACTIVITY BOX 2.1   ADMINISTERING THE CHECKLIST

Introducing the checklist

- Give the pupils some explanation about why they are being presented with the questionnaire. This can be fairly general, e.g. 'We would like to know what happens to people in school. In this booklet are various things that might have happened to you during the last week.'
- Read out at least the first item for the pupils and show them how to complete this. You can read out each item if you prefer. If there are children with a reading age below 8 years, they may need individual assistance.

Achieving the right atmosphere

- Make sure the pupils are working individually and are not overlooked by other pupils. There should be no discussion between pupils whilst the checklist is being completed. Give each pupil as much privacy as possible.

By working out the Bullying Index and General Aggression Index for your school you can get an initial understanding of levels of bullying in your school. After this, you can repeat the checklist after you have intervened, using it like a 'dipstick' to find out whether or not your anti-bullying strategies are working. You will probably see a reduction in the General Aggression Index before the Bullying Index comes down. Use the Index with groups of forty pupils or more, i.e. a whole year group. For groups smaller than forty the Index will not be sufficiently reliable to allow valid comparisons. If you only have small classes, you can calculate the Bullying Index for the whole school.

ACTIVITY BOX 2.2   SCORING THE BULLYING/GENERAL AGGRESSION INDEX

The key items

Item 4: Tried to kick me.

Item 8: Said they'd beat me up.

Item 10: Tried to make me give them money.

Item 24: Tried to hurt me.

Item 37: Tried to break something of mine.

Item 39: Tried to hit me.

The responses to these items will give a quick impression of the extent of bullying in your school.

The Bullying Index

Step 1   For each of the six items, count the number of times that a tick was placed under the category 'more than once'. Do this separately for each of the six key items (Items 4, 8, 10, 24, 37, 39).

Step 2   Divide the scores for each separate item by the number of checklists completed. This will give you the percentage of pupil responses for each item.

Step 3   Add all the six percentages.

Step 4   Divide this number by six. Use two decimal points, e.g. 7.12 or 8.03. This figure is the 'Bullying Index' for your school.

The General Aggression Index

Step 1   For each of the six items, count the number of times that a tick was placed under the category 'more than once'. Do this separately for each of the six key items (Items 4, 8, 10, 24, 37, 39).

Step 2   Divide the scores for each separate item by the number of checklists completed. This will give you the percentage of pupil responses for each item.

Step 3   For each of the six items, count the number of times that a tick was placed under the category 'once'. Do this separately for each of the six key items (Items 4, 8, 10, 24, 37, 39).

Step 4   Divide the scores for each separate item by the number of checklists completed. This will give you the percentage of pupil responses for each item.

Step 5   Add all the twelve percentages.

Step 6   Divide this number by twelve. Use two decimal points, e.g. 15.02 or 20.55. This figure is the 'General Aggression Index' for your school.

Interpreting the results: gender differences

Boys' responses are normally around two or three times as high as girls' responses. This does not necessarily mean that boys are bullied more often than girls. Acts of bullying include a wide variety of behaviours, from very clear physical aggression to more subtle threats of this and on to psychological intimidation, demeaning, social exclusion, etc. Not all these items are included in the checklist. The six items do have a bias towards more physical bullying. Consequently, boys bullying may be detected more easily with the Index than girls. However, physical and non-physical bullying usually coexist, so a high Bullying Index can be interpreted as indicating the likelihood of a high level of bullying all round and vice versa.

For the same reasons, girls who are bullied may not be as readily identified with the six items alone. You may want to look carefully at responses for some other items, e.g. Item 35, 'Laughed at me horribly' or Item 38, 'Told a lie about me'.

Using the checklist to build a comprehensive picture of life in your school

You may wish to look at all the actions on the checklist to obtain a more all-round picture of what happens in school during one week. You can also assess the experiences of individual or small groups of pupils in this way. For the small groups you can work out the percentages of responses to each item on the checklist for each of the two categories 'once' and 'more than once'.

Using the checklist to identify bullied pupils

Any pupil who ticks any of the key items under 'more than once' is more at risk of being bullied. If you want to find out who is being bullied you will need to ask the pupils to put their names on the checklist before they fill it in. This may make some pupils more reluctant to give negative information about themselves.

Using the checklist to gain extra information of your choice

You can use the back page to find out any extra information you feel is important. This might be general information about the pupil, their perceptions of the school or more information about their experience. Make sure that this page can be completed both by pupils who are bullied and by pupils who are not, to avoid drawing attention to the bullied group.

Copyright

There is no copyright on the checklist. Tiny Arora would however appreciate:

- a copy of any results you have obtained by using the checklist;
- a copy of any different version of the checklist which you have made.

Any information received will be treated as confidential. Tiny's address is: Division of Education, University of Sheffield, 388 Glossop Road, Sheffield S10 2JA.

Developing your own survey

There are advantages and disadvantages to developing your own survey.

Advantages

- Pupils can be involved in the design and administration of the questionnaire as well as analysis of the results. This will raise awareness of bullying and enable them to appreciate the effects of it and to take it more seriously.
- The questionnaire can be designed to meet the specific needs of your school.

Disadvantages

- To be sure your questionnaire is good you would need to pilot it and double check it.
- It is difficult to compare your results easily with those of other surveys.
- Analysing the results can be very time consuming.

Things which surveys can identify

In your own survey you can include questions about:

- how often pupils have been bullied;
- the different ways in which they have been bullied;
- how they feel about it;
- if they have told anyone about it;
- how often they have bullied others;
- where the bullying is taking place;
- whether any action is taking place to prevent bullying.

Your own questionnaire can be long or it can be very short. An example of a short questionnaire is included in **Information Box 2.2**.

INFORMATION BOX 2.2   QUICK CHECKS ON BULLYING BEHAVIOUR: AN EXAMPLE OF A QUESTIONNAIRE

How many times have any of these things happened to you during lunchtime today?

TICK:	Did not happen	Once	More than once
I was pushed, kicked or hit on purpose.			
I was threatened.			
Other children told nasty stories about me.			
I had my belongings taken from me.			
I was called nasty names because of my race or colour.			
I was called nasty names for other reasons.			
I was left out on purpose.			
Someone was nasty to me in another way.			

INFORMATION BOX 2.3   TIPS FOR DESIGNING QUESTIONNAIRE
SURVEYS

- If you want to identify specific classes or groups of children experiencing particular problems with bullying, you *will* need to know which class each respondent is in as well as their gender, age and race; these can be filled in at the top of the questionnaire.
- Before they complete the questionnaire, some definition of bullying should be given to make sure that pupils understand what bullying includes.
- If you are asking pupils how often they have been bullied, give a clear time period, for example 'How many times have you been bullied in school, *since the Christmas holidays*?'
- Distinguish between the bullying that occurs in school and bullying that occurs out of school.
- Make the questionnaire as accessible as possible, e.g. large-print versions, translations into community languages, illustrations and pictures.

INFORMATION BOX 2.4   TIPS FOR ADMINISTERING
QUESTIONNAIRE SURVEYS

- The questionnaires should be completed in a quiet atmosphere.
- The instructions should be made very clear (e.g. whether to write answers, tick one box, etc.). Go through one or two opening questions. With younger children or children who may have some learning difficulties you may need to read through each item.
- Emphasise anonymity. Remind pupils that their answers will remain private. You may want someone other than the class teacher or form tutor to administer the questionnaire.
- Maximise privacy. Make sure pupils are not overlooked and discourage discussion between pupils.
- Note who is absent and ask them to complete the questionnaire when they return.
- When repeating a survey, do it at the same time of year. This avoids differences in results due to seasonal variation.

Interviews

By interviewing pupils you can learn more information about bullying behaviour.

Advantages

- You will get richer and more detailed information about bullying in school generally.
- Interviews are more flexible – you can follow up a relevant issue.
- Interviews enable children with moderate or severe learning difficulties to be involved in your survey.
- Group interviews can help pupils to understand the effects that bullying has on other pupils by listening to other pupils' perceptions and may encourage peer support.

Disadvantages

- Pupils may not talk honestly about their own experiences.
- Interviews can be lengthy and time consuming.
- A lot of staff time will be needed when the interviews are conducted on a one-to-one basis.

INFORMATION BOX 2.5   TIPS FOR CONDUCTING INTERVIEWS WITH PUPILS

- Consider who does the interviewing, as the relationship between the interviewer and pupil can affect the honesty of the answers.
- Find a quiet, private place for the interview, preferably without any interruptions.
- When the pupil arrives, greet the pupil warmly, make him or her feel relaxed.
- Explain why they are being interviewed and what the interview will be about.
- Be sensitive to signs of stress in the pupils. Be prepared to spend time counselling the pupil if necessary.
- Do not ask pupils to repeat nasty names they have been called, or stories which have been told about them.
- End the interview on a positive note to deter the negative feelings that may surround the issue of bullying.

ACTIVITY BOX 2.3 IDENTIFYING HIGH-RISK LOCATIONS

Using maps

Supply the pupils with maps of the school (inside and out), and ask them to highlight the places where bullying takes place or where they feel unsafe. Areas which are described as unsafe by more than half the pupils would be viewed as high risk.

Using photographs

Take photographs of different locations in and around your school. Stick them on the wall or on card so that the pupils can see them clearly (level with their line of vision). Underneath each photograph pin up two envelopes, one marked with a happy face and one with an unhappy face. Each pupil is asked to place a counter/token in the happy or unhappy envelope to indicate how she or he feels about each location. Count up the counters/tokens for each envelope. Locations which have been identified as 'unhappy' places by most pupils are likely to be 'high-risk' locations.

ACTIVITY BOX 2.4 IDENTIFYING WHO BULLIES WHO IN YOUR CLASS

Peer nomination

Give each pupil a piece of paper. Ask each pupil to write down the names of three girls and three boys in their class who:

- have a lot of friends;
- are happy in school;
- get picked on a lot by other pupils;
- pick on other pupils a lot.

They can put the same person's name for more than one of the four items.

Take in the papers and make a note of those pupils who were regularly nominated for either or both of the last two items. These pupils are likely to be involved in bullying behaviour.

Individual pupil activities

These activities are designed to find out who has been involved in bullying behaviour or where bullying is happening. This kind of information will help you to target interventions. Most of these activities are manageable on a small scale, i.e. with your class, but impractical on a large scale such as with the whole school.

Measuring bullying over time

Repeated surveys and monitoring let you look at changes in bullying behaviour over time. The frequency of being bullied (though not of bullying others) reduces with age. Expect a reduction of about 15 per cent in levels of pupils reporting being bullied as they progress from one year to the next. Any change over time which is about this level is unlikely to be due to your intervention. It is more accurate to make comparisons over time either on a whole-school basis or between the same year groups (i.e. year nine in the first survey with year nine in the second survey). Report changes as percentages to allow for comparisons between groups of different sizes.

Bullying increases at first as a result of awareness raising. Once staff and pupils begin to discuss bullying behaviour openly, the pupils will be more likely to report it. If the response to these reports continues to be quick and efficient, then over time levels of bullying should fall. If your levels of bullying were high to start with, you might find large drops in levels of bullying in the first year of policy implementation. Bullying, however, may still be above average and you should continue to be active in combating these problems.

SUMMARY

Measuring levels of bullying is a useful and worthwhile way to begin your anti-bullying work. You can be more accurate in understanding bullying behaviour in your school and more precise when intervening. By repeating the measurement at regular intervals you will know how successful you have been in tackling the problem.

My Life in School

You may photocopy this booklet and use it in your school.

I am a boy ☐   **I am a girl** ☐

During this week in school another child:	Not at all	Once	More than once
1. Called me names			
2. Said something nice to me			
3. Was nasty about my family			
4. Tried to kick me			
5. Was very nice to me			
6. Was unkind because I am different			
7. Gave me a present			
8. Said they'd beat me up			
9. Gave me some money			
10. Tried to make me give them money			
11. Tried to frighten me			
12. Asked me a stupid question			
13. Lent me something			
14. Stopped me playing a game			
15. Was unkind about something I did			
16. Talked about clothes with me			
17. Told me a joke			
18. Told me a lie			
19. Got a gang on me			
20. Tried to make me hurt other people			

Age ☐   Year ☐

During this week in school another child:	Not at all	Once	More than once
21. Smiled at me			
22. Tried to get me into trouble			
23. Helped me carry something			
24. Tried to hurt me			
25. Helped me with my class work			
26. Made me do something I didn't want to do			
27. Talked about TV with me			
28. Took something off me			
29. Shared something with me			
30. Was rude about the colour of my skin			
31. Shouted at me			
32. Played a game with me			
33. Tried to trip me up			
34. Talked about things I like			
35. Laughed at me horribly			
36. Said they would tell on me			
37. Tried to break something of mine			
38. Told a lie about me			
39. Tried to hit me			

T·H·R·E·E

how to establish a whole-school anti-bullying policy

SONIA SHARP
DAVID THOMPSON

A whole-school policy should be central to any efforts to tackle the problem of bullying in schools. The anti-bullying policy provides a framework for intervention and prevention and should be an extension of existing behaviour and equal opportunities policy. In this section, we will describe the process of policy development and implementation but first we will establish what an anti-bullying policy is and how it can help your school to tackle bullying behaviour.

What is an anti-bullying policy?

The policy itself is a statement of intent which guides action and organisation within the school. The policy therefore establishes a clear set of agreed aims which provide pupils, staff and parents with a sense of direction and an understanding of the commitment of the school to do something about bullying behaviour. To enable implementation of the policy, the school will define procedures and systems for preventing and responding to bullying. Both the policy and the strategies underpinning it help staff to be consistent in their approach to bullying behaviour and to promote anti-bullying values within the school.

The policy can be implemented at a number of levels. Schools which are attempting to change attitudes and behaviour in their school must make a concerted effort to address the problem in all parts of the school system.

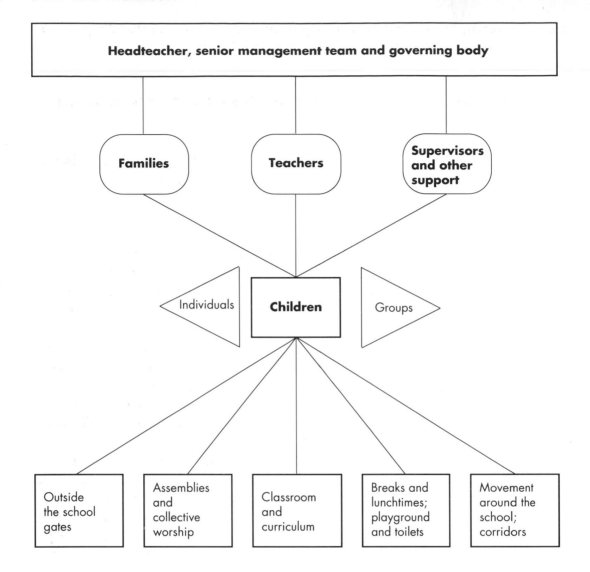

Figure 3.1 Levels of implementation of a whole-school anti-bullying policy

The role of senior management

Headteachers, senior managers and governors must demonstrate commitment to tackling bullying behaviour. This will not only require the allocation of time and resources to the development and implementation of the policy, but also necessitate their direct involvement in the development process; support for other staff during the development process and their management skills in ensuring that the policy is put into practice by all staff (taking prompt action if it is not).

What can we hope to achieve by having a whole-school policy?

Once the school policy is implemented, you should begin to perceive changes in the school culture and in staff, pupil and parent attitudes and behaviour.

Staff

Staff should become more vigilant within the classroom, when moving around the school and when supervising children at play. Incidents which may involve bullying will be followed up quickly; incidents which definitely involve bullying behaviour will be responded to straight away and followed up as appropriate. Staff will always find time to listen to pupils' concerns.

Behaviour management strategies which might humiliate or intimidate pupils will be avoided; rather staff will employ a direct, clear and firm approach which focuses on problem solving and enables the pupils to take an active role in finding a solution to the conflict. Similarly, staff will interact with other staff in a way which demonstrates respect and models positive relationship-building skills. When staff are in conflict with each other, they will try to resolve the difficulties constructively.

In the classroom, there is an emphasis throughout the curriculum on creating a caring community, where pupils and adults are openly valued. Pupils learn to work together in a co-operative manner, to trust, to help and share with each other. They are taught to observe more carefully, communicate needs and wants and listen sensitively. Pupils learn to express their feelings in ways which are not aggressive or destructive and to respect and appreciate differences and similarities and to understand how prejudice works.

When supervising, staff move around the playground area, chatting briefly with pupils. They look out for situations where children seem unhappy and intervene quietly and calmly.

Pupils

Most pupils will feel more confident to tell a member of staff if they are being bullied or if they know that someone else is being bullied. Their peer group culture will value co-operation and tolerance. This does not mean that everyone in a class will be close friends but rather that the individual and friendship groups that do exist do not gain status through aggressive or dominant behaviour. Peer approval will be given for non-aggressive behaviour and unacceptable behaviour such as bullying will meet with rejection or challenge.

Pupils may reject bullying in a fairly passive way by excluding peers when they behave aggressively; by making room in their social group for pupils being bullied; by refusing to join in with bullying behaviour; by non-verbally registering their disapproval and by not ignoring bullying behaviour. They may challenge the behaviour more actively: by calling for help from an adult; by telling the bullying pupils that they don't think what they are doing is fair or by telling them to leave the other person alone; by trying to help the bullied pupil to escape the situation; by taking deliberate steps to prevent contact between the bullying and bullied pupils; by encouraging other peers not to support the pupils who are bullying; by accompanying the bullied pupil to tell a member of staff about the situation; by trying to reduce the likelihood of the bullying recurring. Whatever action is taken, the pupils who have been bullying others are left in no doubt about the disapproval of their peers.

The pupils who spend much of their time in this kind of atmosphere are likely to feel confident and that they do not have to accept bullying behaviour. Pupils who do indulge in bullying behaviour are likely to feel uncomfortable because they are breaking the group norms and also they are unlikely to receive a fearful or satisfactory response from their chosen victim. Pupils being bullied are more likely to actively seek support from their other classmates because they will expect to be supported. The level of sensitivity to different kinds of bullying behaviour is likely to be high – even minor aggressions are more likely to be noticed because this kind of behaviour is not the norm. Thus, the bullying cycle is difficult to establish in the first place and easily interrupted if it begins.

Parents

Most parents will be clear about the school's approach to bullying and will support this by encouraging co-operative behaviour in and around the home. They will be quick to discourage aggressive ways of resolving difficulties. They will immediately inform the school if they suspect their child is being bullied or bullying others. If their child is found to be bullying others, they will work with the school to help their child change their behaviour.

How long does it take to establish a whole-school anti-bullying policy?

The amount of time it will take to develop and implement your whole-school policy will vary depending on how much effort and time you are able to commit to it and what other priorities have been identified by the school.

You should allow a term for planning and preparation. During this initial phase, you will be able to gather materials and resources about bullying; identify where training sessions and consultation meetings will fit into the school calendar; contact helpful people both within and external to the school. Thorough consultation will take approximately a term; once this has been completed, time is needed to collate ideas, to draft and redraft the policy. In the early stages of implementation of the policy, it may require some 'fine tuning' to establish it firmly. The policy should be reviewed annually.

Depending on how thoroughly you have implemented your policy, you should begin to see some changes within the first year. You will usually experience an initial increase in numbers of pupils reporting being bullied. This is due to increased awareness of what bullying is combined with improved confidence in teacher response. The number of bullying situations may not decrease but should certainly be picked up earlier and responded to more efficiently. Over time, levels of bullying *will* decline.

A model for whole-school policy development

The process of policy development can be defined in terms of five distinct stages. These are:

- awareness-raising
- consultation
- preparation of draft and transition to final policy
- communication and implementation
- maintenance and review

Suggestions for how each of these stages can be achieved are detailed in this section. *The process by which the policy is developed is as important as the content of the final policy document and its implementation.*

Awareness-raising

The aim of this aspect of policy development is to inform people about bullying and engage them in discussion so that:

- they have access to up-to-date information about the nature and extent of bullying and can therefore make informed decisions;

- some of the mythology which surrounds the problem of bullying can be dispelled;
- there is some degree of common understanding and agreement about what bullying is.

A helpful starting point for awareness raising and subsequent work on policy development is to consider how bullying can be defined. The activity 'Defining Bullying' (**Activity Box 3.1**) is an effective and discussion-promoting activity to introduce in the early stages of awareness-raising.

The activity can be adapted for use with parents, pupils and governors.

Facts and figures about bullying

To enable people to make informed decisions about the content of the policy as well as to help dispel some of the myths around the problem of bullying, it is helpful to provide some kind of training or information pack which presents current information about the problem of bullying. Data which you have collected about your school can be invaluable at this stage. It is too easy for people to dismiss the problem of bullying by saying: 'It isn't that bad in our school.' All schools have *some* bullying behaviour. If you would like to find out how much bullying goes on in your school, turn to Chapter 2. Chapter 1 provides general information about the problem of bullying.

Awareness-raising training can include:

- reasons why bullying should be tackled and benefits for school effectiveness in reducing bullying;
- the effects of bullying behaviour on children's emotional, physical and psychological health as well as on learning;
- statistics which show general levels of bullying likely in most schools;
- statistics which show the extent of bullying found in your own school;
- information about the general nature of bullying, e.g. gender differences and similarities, types of bullying behaviour, locations which are high risk, school factors, home factors, contexts which encourage/discourage bullying behaviour;
- details of the range of preventative and response strategies available;
- information about what other schools have done.

High-quality training sessions to inform people about bullying can motivate and energise the school community to take action. There may be a small number of adults within your school who do not believe that bullying is a problem, either because they are underestimating the extent of bullying behaviour in your school or because they believe that bullying behaviour is not harmful. Some people even believe that bullying is a helpful part of children's social development. You should aim to convince these people that schools can reduce bullying and that it is worthwhile investing time and resources in doing so.

ACTIVITY BOX 3.1: 'DEFINING BULLYING'

Aims

The purpose of the first part of the activity is to allow individuals to identify for themselves the key features which they personally use to define bullying.

The second part of the activity, the group discussion, aims to enable participants to express, and possibly challenge, their attitudes and values about bullying behaviour. It also illustrates how varied and complex defining bullying can be.

The whole activity facilitates the development of a mutually agreed definition of bullying.

Procedure

Part 1 Initially, participants are asked to work individually to gauge their own first reaction as to whether the incident could be described as bullying or not. Remind participants not to spend ages agonising over each scenario – the situations are brief because often the onlooker, especially the adult onlooker, only catches a tiny fraction of the whole situation. They are also asked to consider how they would react – would they immediately intervene or would they hold back and monitor the situation? Finally, they are asked to reflect on what it was about each of the situations they felt *did* constitute bullying which made them label it as such.

There is usually some degree of individual variation on this. By reflecting on their possible response to each situation, they will be able to identify how seriously they rate different types of bullying behaviour. This is important for deciding on intervention strategies and sanctions during later stages of policy development.

Part 2 The participants then go on to discuss in groups the differences and similarities between their perceptions of the situations. Warn participants that this is likely to lead to debate and that there most probably will be differences of opinion about what is and what is not bullying. The groups are asked to focus on those situations where all participants agree the situation *does* involve bullying behaviour and to note down the key defining features of those situations – from these a consensual definition of bullying can be devised.

With small groups it is possible to continue this activity until a mutual definition is achieved. With larger groups, it may be helpful for notes from each small group to be collated and summarised into a draft definition.

ACTIVITY WORKSHEET 3.1 DEFINING BULLYING

What is bullying?

Consider the following situations and decide whether you feel they constitute bullying or not. Put a 'yes' by the ones you feel are bullying and a 'no' by the ones you feel are not. Be prepared to share your thoughts with other colleagues when you have completed the activity individually.

Don't spend ages agonising over each one!

	Bullying yes or no?
Every time Joanne walks past Serla she gives her hair a little tweak.	
Joel kicks Dean's bag over the floor.	
Tania and Susan won't let Rachel play with them.	
Dean's parents have split up. Mark tells everyone else in the class.	
Rashid and Peter refuse to talk to Ganesh for a week.	
Jenny tells Tony that if he doesn't give her 5p each week she will beat him up.	
Peter tells Thor that if he doesn't do everything he tells him to he will tell the teachers that it was Thor who kicked the ball through the window.	
Tracey knows that Fatima is afraid of spiders. She puts a spider on her hair.	
A group of girls sets fire to Zena's hair because she 'doesn't fit in'.	
Sarah and her family go to church each Sunday. The other children in her class begin to call her 'dirty Christian'.	
John has a disability which means that he cannot always control his movements. When he gets excited his hands jerk up. A group of boys mimic him whenever he tries to join in the football game.	

Dena keeps on telling Susan to wear deodorant.	
Jocelyn has nicknamed Tara 'scruffy'. Now all of the pupils call her that too.	
Terry spits in a can of coke and says he will make Jake drink it.	
Teresa tells the rest of her classmates that Caroline's family eat muck.	
David spends a lunchtime following Simon and tapping him on the arm, despite Simon's requests to be left alone.	
A group of older boys will not let anyone else play football at break. They take the balls away or barge into the other children's games.	
Every time Peter passes a gang of girls they wolf whistle and make comments about his body. One day they grab hold of him and kiss him.	
Each time that Ramon walks into the class a group of pupils giggle and whisper to each other.	

Look over the scenarios you felt definitely were bullying: what are the features of these situations which make you feel this way? These features will provide the basic elements of your personal definition of bullying.

Now consider how you would respond to these situations if you became aware of them as you were moving around the school. Are there some you would immediately react to and others you would perhaps leave this time? The intensity of your reaction will give you an idea of how seriously you rate different kinds of bullying behaviour.

In a group take it in turns to share your responses to the situations. Note any differences and similarities in opinion. It is likely that there will be some differences of opinion about what is bullying and what is not.

Spend the remaining time trying to create a group definition of bullying which clearly describes what you collectively feel bullying is. Be prepared to share your definition with the whole group.

> **INFORMATION BOX 3.1**   COMMON QUESTIONS ABOUT THE
> DEFINITION OF BULLYING
>
> The activity 'defining bullying' usually provokes discussion. Below are some
> of the issues which often arise.
>
> **Persistence**   does it have to happen more than once for the behaviour to
> be classed as bullying? If persistence is an identifying feature of bullying,
> what are the implications of this for sanctions? Is there a distinction
> between the way an adult should respond the first time someone is called a
> nasty name and the second or third time?
>
> **Physical vs psychological intimidation**   should behaviours which
> hurt or frighten people mentally and emotionally be included? How can
> they be identified? How subtle can bullying behaviour be (e.g. a 'look')?
>
> **The relationship between bullying and aggression**   how can we
> distinguish between bullying and non-bullying aggressive behaviour? What
> are the implications of this for the way our anti-bullying policy relates to
> other discipline and behaviour policies?

Consultation

At this stage you will need to ask the different community groups for ideas about
the policy. The wider and more thorough the consultation when devising a policy, the
more likely it is to be successfully implemented. You will need to involve *all* staff
and pupils in the consultation stage; you should aim to include as many families and
governors as possible.

A *multi-disciplinary working party* can help with the organisation of consultation and
the formulation of the draft policy document. Pupils, lunchtime supervisors and parents can be helpfully active within such working parties. Community police officers,
general practitioners and local church figures can provide different perspectives and
help to reinforce the policy once completed. If you are going to establish a working
party, remember that its purpose is to oversee and co-ordinate the policy development
process and it should not *replace* broader consultation. Maintain good communication
links between the working party and the wider community.

School councils, newsletters, family associations and other local committees can be
used to let people know that the school intends to take action against bullying and to
ask them to become involved. Some questions to guide discussion are included in
Activity Box 3.2.

ACTIVITY BOX 3.2   QUESTIONS TO GUIDE CONSULTATION

Questions which can help to guide discussion at the consultation stage include:

- ideally, what would you like to see happening in school about the problem of bullying?
- what should the school policy aim to do?
- whom should it address?
- how can bullying be prevented and discouraged?
- how can we find out if bullying is going on?
- what should be done if bullying behaviour is discovered or reported?
- how will we know whether or not the policy works?

It may be necessary to try more than one method of consultation to achieve thoroughness. Offer opportunities for discussion as well as written consultation. Discussion discourages superficial consultation.

Involving families

Common fears about family involvement include:

'. . . our school will get a reputation for being a bullying school!'

Fact   Active schools are positively viewed by parents and other community figures as being 'schools which do something about bullying'. Policy development enhances their reputation and it has been presented as a reason for parents choosing the school for their children.

'. . . other people who are not teachers don't understand how schools work. They will come up with impractical suggestions!'

Fact   Non-teaching members of the school community often make similar suggestions to teaching staff about ways of combating the problem. Understanding of how schools function and the role of teachers and supervisors is enhanced through working together.

'. . . the parents aren't interested. It would be a waste of time.'

Fact   Many parents are concerned about the issue of bullying. One benefit of involvement of parents in policy development is enhanced home–school communication.

INFORMATION BOX 3.2 SOME WAYS OF INVOLVING FAMILIES

You can involve families through:

- home visits (by staff or by other agencies, such as an educational welfare officer);
- newsletters or questionnaires;
- use of community meetings or noticeboards, e.g. religious services, library, shop and post office notices, playgroups, community projects, GP's waiting room;
- family evenings;
- events where family turn-out is high, e.g. plays, fetes, jumble sales, concerts;
- collection points for children, e.g. at the school gate;
- informal or formal contact between families and school, e.g. a family phones to say that their child is unwell – the person who takes the call can inform the parent about the policy development and encourage them to participate;
- events/meetings in other cluster schools where families may also be involved.

Record which families have been contacted to enable targeting of uninvolved parents.

Involving staff

Teaching and non-teaching staff should be included in the consultation process. It is very important to involve lunchtime supervisors. Most bullying takes place around the school, therefore adults who are supervising breaks and lunchtimes need to know how to identify bullying and how to respond to it.

Senior managers should direct *all* staff to take an active role in the consultation process. A quick glance over a draft document is not sufficient. Staff should be purposefully involved in discussion about the school's anti-bullying approach.

Involving pupils

Pupil involvement is extremely important as peer pressure is a powerful force for tackling bullying. Consultation with pupils can take place in tutorial time or lesson time. Give the pupils time to talk about what they think bullying is as well as what the school should be doing about bullying.

ACTIVITY BOX 3.3   QUESTIONS FOR DISCUSSION WITH PUPILS

How can we make our school a safer place?

How can we stop bullying?

- in the playground?
- in the classroom?
- in the corridors and toilets?
- at lunchtimes and breaktimes?
- outside school?

How can we make it easier for pupils to tell an adult if they are being bullied?

What should teachers and other adults do if someone is being bullied?

- to help the bullied pupil?
- to help the bullying pupils?

What can you and other pupils do about bullying?

You may wish to develop individual class anti-bullying charters with the pupils. Any policy work should emphasise how important every pupil is in relation to reducing bullying behaviour. Emphasise the role of the bystander in policy development and reinforce it through curriculum work on bullying (see Chapter 4).

Preparation of the draft policy and transition from draft to final policy

At this stage all the ideas which have arisen in the consultation stage need to be pulled together to form a draft document. This needs to be recirculated to all the consulted groups for comment and change. *It is recommended that this recirculation includes an opportunity for discussion as well as written comment.* The inclusion of parents, pupils, non-teaching staff and governors as well as teaching staff is vital.

When devising your policy, you will need to consider:

1 The aims of the policy

- What do you want to achieve?
- When do you want to achieve this by?
- Are your aims realistic?

2 A clear definition of bullying behaviour

- What is bullying?
- Are some kinds of bullying worse than others?
- How is bullying different from other kinds of aggressive behaviour?
- Is there a difference between adults bullying each other and children bullying each other?
- How do children bully adults? How do adults bully children?

3 Strategies for prevention of bullying

- How can we teach children not to bully?
- How can we encourage co-operative behaviour?
- How can we make sure that particularly 'at risk' groups of pupils have access to this teaching (e.g. pupils with learning difficulties; pupils who do not speak or understand English fluently)?
- What kinds of anti-bullying attitudes and values do we want to promote within the school? How shall we achieve this?
- How can teachers and other staff show pupils non-bullying ways of resolving conflict?

4 Reporting bullying

- How should pupils report bullying (to whom, when, how)?
- How can we make sure this system is manageable by staff?
- What should we record?
- Who is responsible for co-ordinating the recording system?
- How will this information be used?
- What action will follow a report of bullying?
- How can we check for false allegations?

5 Responding to bullying (see Chapter 5 for more detailed advice)

- Who should respond (adults, pupils)?
- How should they respond immediately?
- What follow-up action is required?
- Do we need different responses for different kinds of bullying?
- How can we support the bullied pupils in a way which will help them feel strong and powerful?
- How should we differentiate between responses to name-calling or teasing, and bullying which leads to physical assault?
- How shall we know whether or not the bullying has stopped?

- What shall we do if the bullying persists?
- At what stage should we involve parents? How shall we do this?
- What should we record? How will this information be used?

6 Roles and responsibilities of teachers, non teaching staff, pupils, parents and governors in implementing the policy

- What will this policy look like in practice?
- What changes will we have to make to our classroom practice; to our break and lunchtime management systems; to our own behaviour?
- How much time and which resources are necessary for this policy to work? Where shall we find them?
- Which staff already have specific skills which will help with the implementation of this policy?
- What specific training needs do other staff and pupils have?

7 Monitoring and evaluating the policy

- How shall we know whether the policy is working?
- What information do we need?
- How shall we collect it?
- Who will be involved in doing this?
- Who will co-ordinate this process?
- What shall we do if it is not working?

The policy will need to be written in appropriate language for the audience. The key messages in the policy need to be accessible to all members of the school community. It may take several revisions of the policy to arrive at a final policy. Once the policy has been finally agreed, it must be communicated and put into action.

Communication and implementation

The implementation of the policy may involve changes in the way the school is organised and managed. We recommend that careful planning of how and when this is to be achieved is carried out by the working party and management of the school (if they are not involved in the working party already). *The commitment of management is vital at this stage.*

Training

Staff within the school may have specific training needs which must be met before the policy can be implemented. These training needs might include behaviour management skills; counselling skills; assertiveness techniques.

Communication

Initially, you may wish to hold some kind of launch which would involve the whole school community and possibly other groups as well. By giving the policy a high profile the school can emphasise the importance it places upon it. It also encourages less involved people to increase their contact with the policy.

The policy document itself can be included in school handbooks, newsletters. It can be displayed on walls in classrooms and entrance halls. It can be available in waiting areas not only in the school but in local amenities too. Local press and media can be asked to publicise it.

Monitoring

To continue to tackle bullying effectively, your school will need to keep a close check on incidents of bullying behaviour. You will need to develop a system for recording any bullying incidents which occur and how they were responded to and followed up. Any recording system will need to be implemented by *all* staff in the school not just teaching staff. Some staff may need regularly reminding of this. Relevant information about pupils who are causing concern must be accessible to staff throughout the school as bullying behaviour may disappear in one sector of the school, only to reappear in another. Don't forget to double check your monitoring system every so often – lack of records may mean that no-one is using it!

One method of double-checking is to introduce an interim monitoring system. This might involve a termly mini-survey (see Chapter 2) which could be run by staff, parents or pupils and which would indicate levels of bullying behaviour. These should match with the information in the incident-recording system. If there is a large discrepancy then there is need to re-examine your policy and practice.

Over time, you will learn more about the nature of bullying behaviour in your school. Sometimes levels of bullying will rise dramatically in a particular class or year group or a particular form of bullying will become more prevalent. You will be able to respond to these situations directly.

Maintenance and review

An anti-bullying policy is a long-term commitment. To maintain its effectiveness you will need to regularly remind staff and pupils about it. You also need to identify how well it is working.

> **INFORMATION BOX 3.3**   EXAMPLES OF CURRICULUM THEMES
> WHICH CAN BE USED TO PROMOTE CO-OPERATIVE BEHAVIOUR
>
> - conflict resolution
> - friendship skills
> - negotiating
> - assertiveness training
> - tackling prejudice
> - anger management
> - bullying at work

Maintenance

Some teaching staff may be worried about over publicising the bullying policy, especially if a major launch had marked the initial implementation of the policy. However, a low profile policy is soon forgotten.

We recommend that the policy is referred to more than once each half term. This can be achieved via assemblies, tutorial work and through pupil involvement. Posters referring to the school's commitment to anti-bullying can be regularly changed to maintain interest. The pastoral curriculum can tackle bullying behaviour from a variety of aspects. Try to establish an ongoing programme of strategies to promote co-operative behaviour. The curriculum is an excellent vehicle for achieving this.

New staff, pupils and parents will need opportunities to learn about the policy – this should be more than by inclusion of the policy document in the school handbook. To emphasise its importance it will need to be commented on and discussed. Your staff need to feel confident in their ability to broach the subject of bullying with pupils and to respond to it when it occurs.

Review

It is important to know whether or not the policy is being implemented successfully. Regular dates for review are essential and this process should provide opportunities for all staff and pupils to comment on the success of the policy in practice.

As well as individuals' perceptions of how well the policy is working, use the information gathered through monitoring to provide factual indicators of success. Some indicators you might use are included in **Information Box 3.4.**

INFORMATION BOX 3.4   POSSIBLE INDICATORS OF CHANGE

- reduction in levels of reported bullying
- reduced duration of bullying incidents
- increased willingness to 'tell' of bullying (by bullied pupils, their parents or by bystanders)
- improved attendance
- enhanced pupil achievement
- more parents opting to send their child to your school.

Don't be disappointed if in the first year you only see small changes – major change takes time to achieve. You should, however, be able to identify *some* change. You should at least experience an increase in numbers of pupils who will tell a teacher if they or a peer is being bullied. You should also find a reduction in the duration of bullying when it does occur. If after two years you are still not finding signs of an improved social climate within your school, then you will need to examine your policy carefully and how it is being put into practice around the school.

Remember to let governors, staff, parents and pupils know how you have been successful in achieving change. This will encourage continued effort to tackle the problem. Don't ignore difficulties or lack of change identified by the review – feed this information back to the school community as a collective problem to be solved and look for constructive solutions.

A final word . . .

The process of policy development is as important as its implementation and review – don't be tempted to cut corners. Establishing a whole-school anti-bullying policy is a worthwhile but energy consuming activity. Be patient and maintain your motivation for change. We hope you will be able to use some of the ideas and advice given in this section to guide you in establishing your school anti-bullying policy. Schools *can* reduce levels of bullying behaviour and having an effective policy is an essential first step.

F·O·U·R

how to tackle bullying through the curriculum

HELEN COWIE
SONIA SHARP

Through curriculum work on bullying, schools can achieve two very important objectives. First, they can raise awareness amongst pupils about bullying behaviour. If a school is about to develop a whole-school policy on the issue, this is an essential early step. If the school already has a whole-school policy on the issue, this is vital for introducing the policy to new pupils and for keeping the policy alive for existing pupils. Second, they can challenge attitudes about bullying behaviour, increase understanding for bullied pupils, and help build an anti-bullying ethos in the school. Whilst curriculum work is unlikely to achieve long-term changes on its own, it has a key role to play here.

There are a wide range of resources available to schools for curriculum-based work on bullying (see Chapter 8). These include videos, plays, poetry and fiction. Alison Skinner's (1992) *Bullying: an annotated bibliography* provides an excellent overview of these. There are also organisations such as the National Association for Pastoral Care in Education which, in conjunction with the Calouste Gulbenkian Foundation, have set up a library of materials relating to bullying behaviour.

Materials for awareness-raising can be used as the basis for discussion, drama, role-play and creative writing about bullying behaviour. They can be used to explore issues such as:

- What is bullying?
- What causes people to bully each other?
- How does it feel to be bullied/to bully?

- What are the effects of bullying behaviour on bullied pupils; on pupils who bully others; on bystanders?
- What would our school and our society be like if bullying behaviour was acceptable?
- Why should we try not to bully each other?
- What can we do to stop bullying?
- Which moral dilemmas do we face when we encounter bullying behaviour?

To *raise awareness* about bullying behaviour and the school's anti-bullying policy requires probably between two and three hours of curriculum time in any year. However, to *maintain awareness and to challenge and change behaviour or attitudes* teachers will need to put in a more prolonged and intensive effort. They will need to reinforce anti-bullying messages regularly throughout the school year and make bullying an ongoing theme in lessons and assemblies. Using teaching methods which actively promote co-operative behaviour and citizenship is one way of achieving this.

In this chapter, we will present three curriculum-based methods for tackling bullying:

- *Quality Circles* – a participative problem-solving approach originating from industry;
- *role-play and drama* – ideas for activities and improvisations;
- *literature, discussion-based activities and creative writing* – ideas for groups and individuals.

Quality circles

What are Quality Circles?

A Quality Circle (QC) is a group of between five and twelve people who meet together on a regular basis, usually weekly, to try to identify ways of improving their organisation. They aim to increase general effectiveness and find solutions to common social and practical problems. To achieve this, the QC uses a structured participative problem-solving process.

The problem-solving process involves the five steps shown in **Information Box 4.1**.

Why use QCs to tackle bullying?

Bullying is a social problem. Pupils who are not directly involved in bullying themselves are still likely to know who is involved in bullying others, who is regularly bullied and where and when it happens. Quality Circles provide a structure for all pupils to apply to the problem of bullying. Through the quality circle process, pupils devise their own solutions to the problem of bullying. They also learn more about

---

INFORMATION BOX 4.1   FIVE STEPS IN PROBLEM-SOLVING

- Identifying the problem
- Analysing the problem
- Developing solutions
- Presenting solutions to 'management'
- Reviewing the solutions

---

the nature of the problem. This process motivates peer pressure against bullying and is a powerful preventative measure.

Bullying is perceived as a real problem in many schools and we have found an enthusiastic response to the QC idea from teachers anxious to incorporate their school anti-bullying policy into lessons. The existence of bullying behaviour in class-room or playground presents challenging opportunities for pupils to make observations, to collect data, to design solutions and to communicate ideas both within the circle and to adults who are in a position to implement reasonable suggestions.

This is important at a number of levels. It gives pupils the chance to make changes in their own environment, and to practise and model pro-social behaviour. It has the potential for enabling children to rehearse responsible roles, which will be valuable throughout their educational and vocational experience. It may well reduce the incidence of bullying in the school.

Who can be involved in a QC?

The aim of the QC is to involve pupils – from 7 years upwards – in devising practical solutions to the problem of bullying. Each QC will consist of between five and twelve pupils. The younger the pupils, the smaller the QC should be. One class of thirty pupils could be divided into five QCs. You will need to make your own decisions about whether pupils can choose who is in their QC or not.

How much time does it take?

Once pupils have formed a QC, it can run indefinitely – meeting once a week throughout each term. It will take a term to complete one cycle of the QC thoroughly, allowing one hour of classtime per week (see **Information Box 4.2**).

INFORMATION BOX 4.2   SAMPLE TIMETABLE FOR QC WORK

Spring Term 1995:   Tuesdays 9.30 am to 10.30 am

Session 1   Introduce concept of QCs to the whole class. Allocate pupils to groups. Begin with QC groups developing logo design and naming of QC. A trust-building activity will help the process of forming the group, so too will the first group activity – designing a logo and deciding on a name for the group.

Session 2   Introduce brainstorming rules. Practice brainstorming as whole class then in individual groups on theme of 'What makes me unhappy in school?' Problem prioritising and voting to agree on one problem area for focus of QC work. 'Identifying group roles' activity.

Session 3   Introduce WHY? WHY? Practice as whole class then in individual QCs using problem agreed last session. Whole-class discussion about research techniques. QCs make plans of how they will collect data about their problem. Evaluation telegrams: 'I feel that this session . . .'.

Session 4   Share observation schedules/questionnaires as whole class and discuss best features. In QCs, finalise design and preparation of survey materials or observation schedules. Develop implementation plans for investigation procedures – what will they do? when? how long do they need? development of materials? what else will they need? do they need to make any special arrangements with other staff? how will they do this? Each QC makes short presentation to rest of class about their plan. Individual evaluation: personal strengths and weaknesses. (Implementation of data collection during week.)

Session 5   Working in QCs: analysis and summary of data. What have they learned from their investigations? How will they present the data?

Session 6   Introduce HOW? HOW? to whole class. QCs try method out to develop own solutions to the problem they are working on and then make an action plan. Evaluation: how we work well together/identifying other people's skills.

Session 7   Give introduction to presentation skills and go through presentation checklist. QCs develop presentation of problem and solution for next session (5 minutes per QC).

Session 8 Practice presentations to whole class. Personal evaluation forms. Other pupils devise questions to ask each QC about their presentation, to enable practice of question handling. (Invite headteacher and governors to next session.)

Session 9 Formal presentations and discussion of QC suggestions. Headteacher and governors discuss suggestions and prepare feedback for each QC.

Session 10 Each QC receives feedback and discusses it amongst themselves. They then complete group evaluation: 'Outcomes of QC work' and decide what they will do next. If suggestions to be implemented, arrange individual QC appointments with headteacher to discuss how this will happen and when.

Session 11 Recap on whole process with whole class. QCs begin to work independently on next problem. Devise own time scale and present to teacher. Evaluation: what we have learned about ourselves and how we will apply this to future QC time.

What skills do the children learn?

The Quality Circle process requires children to:

- work co-operatively with other people;
- express their own thoughts and opinions clearly;
- listen carefully to others;
- keep records of discussions;
- identify and prioritise problems faced by themselves and their peers;
- investigate the extent, causes and effects of the problem;
- analyse their findings;
- formulate solutions;
- evaluate advantages and disadvantages, costs and practical implications of putting any solution into practice;
- present their solutions in a persuasive way.

What materials are needed?

Almost all of the QC techniques require only paper, pens and pencils. Tape measures or stop watches might be needed for the investigatory stage. Access to model-making materials, colourful pens, glue, high quality paper, word processors are helpful but not essential.

How do I start up QCs?

There are two alternative ways of introducing the idea of QCs to your pupils. First, take the pupils through the process a step at a time as a whole class, allowing them to carry out each step in their smaller QC groups before introducing the next step to the whole group. Second, introduce the idea of QCs to the whole class, but then circulate from group to group, teaching each QC the technique they will need next as they progress through the cycle.

The first time a QC meets it has to form as a group and establish an identity. Each QC should decide on a personal name and design a logo to represent itself. You may want to spend time on other trust-building and team-building activities, especially if the members of the QC are not used to working with each other.

Whether in friendship groups or not, each QC has to differentiate itself from the other QCs. This process is begun by naming the QC and designing a distinctive badge or logo. Having a team name gives a group its own identity and makes it unique. The name chosen by the group can reflect some of the interests which group members have in common, it can reflect differences among them, or anything which the QC thinks appropriate. Each group spends some time developing its own name and logo. This can be done in a number of ways (see **Activity Box 4.1**).

The Quality Circle process

Figure 4.1 shows the process of the QC. It is a cycle with five distinct steps. In this section we give an overview of the process and describe some of the practical activities which can be included at each stage.

Step 1 identifying the problem

The QC makes a list of all the problems the group wants to tackle relating to bullying. Once this list is complete, the participants have to decide which problem they are going to address first. They could choose the most serious problem – or they might prefer to choose a problem which is more easily solved before attempting a difficult one.

Problem identification and selection procedures include: brainstorming (**Activity Box 4.2**) and voting procedures (**Activity Box 4.3**).

ACTIVITY BOX 4.1   NAMING THE QC

Brainstorming   The QC brainstorms words which have to do with, for example, the season of the year, the area where they live, the environment around the school. They then discuss a possible name based on the brainstorm.

Open-ended discussion   The QC explores things which they have in common. (This will have been established during the trust-building exercises.) These might include sport, music, animals, hobbies. Building on their commonalities, the QC chooses a name.

Reflecting back   After one member of the QC has put forward an idea for the QC name, the next person must repeat it before going on to make their own suggestion. This helps to ensure that each person is heard and plays a part in the final decision.

Round Robin consensus   QC members generate a variety of possible team names. Using the Round Robin structure, members then vote for a name other than their own, repeating this process, if necessary, until one name receives support from all members.

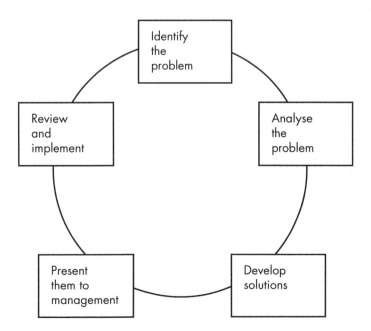

Figure 4.1 The Quality Circle process

ACTIVITY BOX 4.2   BRAINSTORMING

Aim   To enable members of a QC to identify features of school life which they find problematic.

Materials   Large sheets of paper, thick felt pens.

Procedure   One member of the QC acts as scribe. Each group member takes it in turn to suggest an area of concern relating to bullying which they would like to address within the quality circle. The scribe makes a note of these suggestions. It is important that the ideas are not discussed at this stage and especially that there are no negative comments or gestures. Encourage the pupils to be as creative and diverse as they like in their ideas. When a pupil has run out of ideas they can 'pass'. The activity continues until all group members pass.

ACTIVITY BOX 4.3   VOTING PROCEDURES

Aim   To enable pupils to prioritise a problem area to work on during a QC cycle.

Materials   Suggestions generated through brainstorm, pen.

When all the suggestions have been discussed to ensure that everyone is clear about what they mean, then the voting to identify a starting point for the QC can begin. There are two basic ways of doing this:

- Each pupil has three votes. There is a show of hands for each suggestion and the one with the most votes wins. If there is a tie, then each person has one vote and the process is repeated.
- Each pupil rates each suggestion on a scale of 1 to 3, where 1 equals 'not very important to me' and 3 equals 'very important to me'. The scores for each suggestion are collected and added up. The suggestion with the highest score is the priority problem. As before, if two or more problems have the highest score, then the procedure is repeated.

The unselected suggestions are stored carefully; when the QC has worked through the first problem, they will return to the list to consider whether there are any more problems to add and which problem they are going to address next.

Step 2 Analysis of the problem

Here members of the QC consider possible causes of the problem, breaking it down so that contributing factors are identifiable. The QC then has to decide which causes are the most important. A technique for doing this is shown in the Why? Why? diagram (**Figure 4.2**).

ACTIVITY BOX 4.4   THE WHY? WHY? DIAGRAM

Aim   To explore causes of chosen problem.

Materials   Lots of paper (wallpaper is ideal), pen.

Procedures   At the far left hand side of the paper, the problem is written down (see **Figure 4.2** for an example). The group ask themselves just one question: 'Why?' At this point several possible causes may be identified. These should all be noted down on the first branch of the Why? Why? diagram. The group then ask 'Why?' of each first-level reason and continue to do so until an original causal factor is identified.

Members adopt three distinct roles in the exercise:

- **the inquirer** whose task is to keep asking the question 'Why?' until the line of enquiry can go no further;
- **the respondent** whose task is to provide answers to the question 'Why?';
- **the observers** whose task is to note down all the answers which are produced.

The activity goes through three steps:

- the QC begins with a solution statement and the enquirer explores possible ways of accomplishing the action at each stage by asking 'Why?';
- at each step of the chain, a convergent process can be used to narrow the list of alternatives before the next divergent step is taken;
- after this procedure has been carried out a number of times, the QC discuss which causes seem to be the most significant.

As with all these QC activities, creative thinking should be encouraged. Sometimes ideas which seem bizarre at first can yield helpful information.

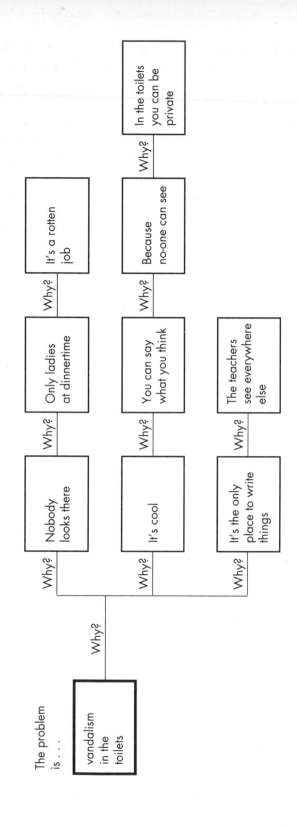

Figure 4.2 Why? Why? Diagram

Having considered possible causes, the group then investigates the problem – trying to find out as much factual information as possible about it (see **Activity Box 4.5**). This part of the QC process is very important. If effective solutions are to be developed, the QC needs maximum information about the nature of the problem – whom it affects, how often it happens, where it happens, for how long it has been happening. When things happen that we don't like we can sometimes over-exaggerate to ourselves the extent of the problem; on the other hand, sometimes what looks on the surface to be a small problem, can turn out to be much more serious than we suspected. In the final stage, when the problem and solutions are presented to the management group, this information can be used to demonstrate that the problem really does exist and that it is worth doing something about.

Useful techniques at this point might include carrying out a survey (e.g. of name-calling at playtime), interviewing a sample of children about their experiences of being bullied, or making selected observations during an agreed time-slot (e.g. between 12.00 and 1.00 pm on a Friday) of behaviour in a particular area of the play-ground (e.g. on the playing field).

Having decided what data are to be collected, the QC needs to agree on the method of data collection. There are two main data collection methods. These are observation schedules and surveys/interviews (see **Activity Boxes 4.6 and 4.7**).

ACTIVITY BOX 4.5   DATA COLLECTION

Aim   To collect objective information about the nature and extent of the problem.

Materials   Paper, pens, possibly tape-recorder or camera.

Procedure   The QC first needs to decide what kinds of information will be needed. This will vary according to the problem, but it might be helpful to consider the following checklist of possible questions:

- Who is involved? (people who are causing the problem, people affected by the problem, people who know about the problem)
- Where is it happening?
- When is it happening?
- What else is happening before, after and during the occurrence of the problem?
- How often is it happening?
- How does it make people feel?
- What are the consequences (immediately, over a long period of time, indirectly)?

ACTIVITY BOX 4.6 OBSERVATION SCHEDULES

Aim   To collect data which will identify the extent and nature of the problem.

Materials   Paper, pens (possibly clipboards, stopwatch).

Procedure   The QC members make a list of important features of the problem which can be seen, heard or felt. They then need to decide when, where and how often they are going to look out for the items on their schedule. They can record objectively (when they are not directly involved in the situation) or subjectively (when they record each time they personally experience something).

It is not practical to observe everything, everywhere, all the time. The pupils will need to decide on a reasonable *sample* for their observations.

This could be *random* (observing on a randomly selected day each week for a month); *consecutive* (every day for a week at 10.30 at the same place); or *stratified* (organised so that the potential range of possible people and places are included, e.g. twenty pupils from each year group, equally split for gender and race, keep personal schedules).

ACTIVITY BOX 4.7 SURVEYS/INTERVIEWS

Aim   To collect data which will identify the extent and nature of the problem.

Materials   Paper, pens (possibly tape-recorders).

Procedures   The pupils devise a questionnaire schedule – a set of questions – which will allow them to find out about the extent of the problem and how it affects people. The questionnaire will need to be tried out first to make sure it can be understood and that the questions are relevant: sometimes a question which seems perfectly logical to the person asking the question, means something completely different to the people being interviewed. The final questionnaire can be given to people individually to complete themselves or can be used as a basis for an interview. If an interview is being used, the pupils need to decide whether they are going to record the information themselves by hand or use tape. They also need to consider how many people they want to interview and who these people should be.

Whether the information collected is from schedules, interviews or questionnaires, it needs to be put together in a way which helps the QC to see any patterns, for example, by adding up the number of people who gave each type of answer, or the number of times different types of incident happened. Then the pupils will need to look at the figures and ask themselves 'What does this information tell us about the problem?'

Step 3   developing a solution

Once a cause has been identified and analysed the circle members begin to suggest solutions. The How? How? technique is useful in exploring alternative solutions to a problem. (See **Activity Box 4.8** below and **Figure 4.3**.)

ACTIVITY BOX 4.8   THE HOW? HOW? DIAGRAM

Aim   To generate a range of possible solutions to a problem.

Materials   Lots of paper (wallpaper is ideal), pen.

Procedure   Once a cause has been identified and analysed the circle members begin to suggest solutions. The How? How? technique is useful in exploring alternative solutions to a problem. This time the QC members keep asking the question 'How?' to every solution that is suggested until it culminates in some practical action that can be taken. If it doesn't, then the idea is abandoned.

The How? How? diagram creates a 'means–end chain' which allows QC members a creative opportunity to explore and consider numerous alternatives instead of jumping to an obvious solution. In this way it actually facilitates divergent thinking. At the same time, the structure of the How? How? diagram demonstrates the steps which QC members have to go through in order to implement their solution. Thus it enables them to formulate a specific action plan.

 The procedure is very similar to the Why? Why? diagram described in **Activity Box 4.4**. The QC now brainstorms potential solutions and notes them down. Some of these will be appropriate, others will not. At this stage it does not matter. In a brainstorm, all ideas are noted! The procedure is simple but it is important to stress that no discussion is necessary at this point.

Members adopt three distinct roles in the exercise:

• **the inquirer** whose task is to keep asking the question 'How?' until the line of enquiry can go no further;

- **the respondent** whose task is to provide answers to the question 'How?';
- **the observers** whose task is to note down all the answers which are produced.

The activity goes through three steps:

- the QC begins with a solution statement and the inquirer explores possible ways of accomplishing the action at each stage by asking 'How?';
- at each step of the chain, a convergent process can be used to narrow the list of alternatives before the next divergent step is taken;
- after this process has been carried out a number of times, the QC lists advantages and disadvantages, chance of success and relative cost of each alternative in order to facilitate a more objective selection process.

Some 'How?'s will amount to nothing or will be beyond the means of the pupils or the school. Others, however, will be very appropriate and by tracing the steps back along the How? How? diagram, a clear plan of action should emerge.

An alternative to the HOW? HOW? is Forcefield Analysis. (See **Activity Box 4.9.**)

Once a solution has been agreed a small pilot run is often useful to make sure it works in practice. Preventative measures can also be devised to make sure the problem stays solved.

Step 4   *Presenting a solution*

The QC members prepare a presentation of their solution to a 'management team' (see **Activity Box 4.10**) who facilitate the implementation of the solution if possible.

The pupils need to be encouraged to prepare their presentation well. In particular they need to attend to the content of the talk, making sure their messages are put across clearly and succinctly. They will need to rehearse their presentation and practise speaking directly to the audience, without notes, sounding confident and clear. They will need to consider what visual aids they are going to use to support their presentation – role-play, graphs and charts, summary sheets. Finally, they need to be prepared to handle questions from the management team. (See **Activity Box 4.11.**)

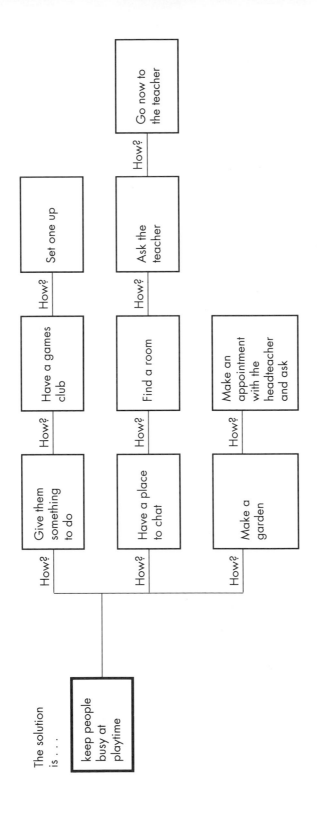

The solution is . . .

keep people busy at playtime

How? — Give them something to do — How? — Have a games club — How? — Set one up

How? — Have a place to chat — How? — Find a room — How? — Ask the teacher — How? — Go now to the teacher

How? — Make a garden — How? — Make an appointment with the headteacher and ask

Figure 4.3 How? How? Diagram

ACTIVITY BOX 4.9 FORCEFIELD ANALYSIS

Aim To develop a set of solutions to a problem by identifying the positive and negative factors in a situation.

Materials Paper, pen.

Procedure The QC members write the problem in the centre of a sheet of paper. Generating upwards from the problem, they note down the helping factors – the things which make it better or which might help to change the situation. They give an idea of the relative power of these forces by drawing arrows of different lengths. A very long arrow would indicate that the force was strong. A short arrow would show that the factor was only small in affecting the situation. Going downwards from the problem they note the barriers or hindrances to the problem – the things that keep it as it is or prevent any change from occurring. Again, the strength of these forces is shown by the length of the arrows.

The group then consider all of the forces. Of the helping, positive forces they ask themselves: 'What could we do to increase or build on this force?' Of the negative, hindering forces they ask themselves: 'What can we do to reduce the effect of this force?' There will be some forces which it is not practical to change. That is OK. Don't waste time on those forces but rather concentrate time and effort on those which *can* be changed. Once each force has been considered in this way, the QC should have a number of strategies – some which address the hindering forces and some which increase the positive forces – which collectively will form an action plan for the problem resolution.

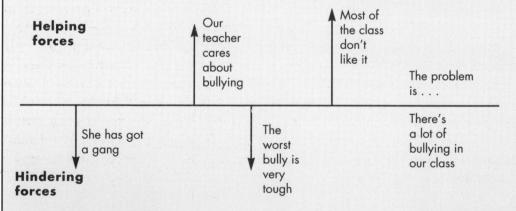

Figure 4.4 A forcefield anaylsis diagram (the pupils must now find ways of strengthening the helping forces and weakening the hindering forces)

ACTIVITY BOX 4.10   FORMING THE MANAGEMENT TEAM

Decide on membership of the management group in advance and approach them before the QC work begins. You may wish to include the headteacher, governors, other staff or pupils. They will need to be carefully briefed on their role. They must be prepared to consider the pupils' solutions seriously and be prepared to facilitate their implementation if they are approved. If they have reservations about their solutions, they should discuss these with the QC and perhaps ask them to revise their solution accordingly.

   The presentation is an important point in the QC cycle. If the pupils feel that their work is seen as 'token', they are unlikely to maintain enthusiasm about QCs.

Step 5   Reviewing the solution

If the management team decide to implement the proposed solution, they must evaluate how effective this solution has been and feed this back to the QC. If the solution is not implemented, there must be discussion between the management group and the QC about the reasons for this decision. The members of the QC can then review and modify their solutions or can move on to another area for concern.

Keeping the QCs healthy

Group dynamics can often be complicated. The QCs will be working together intensively for at least a term, actively involved in a challenging process. There are bound to be differences of opinion amongst the group members and clashes of personality, so it is helpful for pupils to learn how to cope with controversy and disagreement within the group. By evaluating their contributions to the QC meetings, pupils not only enhance communication and problem-solving skills but also have the opportunity to reflect on interpersonal relationships and the emotions which are aroused when people are actively engaged with one another. **Activity Box 4.12** describes eight techniques for developing this reflective capacity by extending the language which pupils have for recounting events, expressing feelings and describing relationship processes. You can include personal and group evaluation procedures at regular intervals within the QC process.

ACTIVITY BOX 4.11   PRESENTATION PREPARATION CHECKLIST

Structure

- Do you begin well?
- What are the key points you want to make?
- Are they in the right order?
- Have you 'signposted' them?
- Do they need some visuals?
- Do you end well?

Style of delivery

- Can you give your talk without reading from notes?
- Are you going to sit or stand?
- Where are you going to look?
- Have you remembered to smile when appropriate?
- Are your visual aids in the right order?

Visual aids

- Are your visual aids clear and simple?
- Are they colourful?
- Do they add to your presentation?
- Do they give information?
- Are they in the right order?
- Have you checked that you know how to work any technical equipment (e.g. tape-recorders, VCRs, OHPs)?

Question handling

- Are you confident about answering any questions which may arise?
- Have you practised answering awkward questions?
- Can you imagine what the panel might ask?
- Do you think you can answer clearly?
- Are there experts in the QC who can help you out?

INFORMATION BOX 4.3   CASE STUDY

One QC selected the problem of boredom at playtime as their area for concern (Step 1). They surveyed their peer group to identify how many children felt bored at lunchtime/playtime and to gather ideas about popular games/activities (Step 2).

From this survey, they found that many pupils complained that the lunch hour was too long and expressed a wish for someone to organise active games. The QC came up with a plan – a lunchtime games tournament for different aged pupils (Step 3).

They worked out a precise plan for organising and administering the tournament, even suggesting ways in which money could be raised to supply small items of equipment such as balls and skipping ropes. They themselves volunteered to run the sessions. They presented their plan to their teacher and headteacher (Step 4).

The headteacher was very impressed by their idea and discussed it at the next teaching staff meeting and with lunchtime supervisors. A few minor organisational adjustments were made based on the headteacher's comments and the lunchtime initiative was introduced, jointly run by pupil 'play monitors' and a lunchtime supervisor. An evaluative questionnaire was completed by staff and pupils at the end of the year. The results were discussed at management meetings (Step 5) and it was decided to keep the sessions going.

Drama and role-play

The power of drama

Drama and role-play help pupils to explore the problem of bullying from a range of perspectives in a purposeful way. To be most effective, the drama and role-play should lead to small group or whole group discussion about the issues and feelings which emerge through the work. Through drama and discussion pupils can examine:

- personal experiences;
- motivation to bully;
- consequences of bullying behaviour;
- the impact of bullying on family, bullied person, bullying person, bystander, teacher;
- ways of stopping bullying behaviour.

ACTIVITY BOX 4.12   REFLECTING ON AN EXPERIENCE

Telling the story

At its most basic level the QC members are given the opportunity to re-tell an experience as it happened to them. Open-ended questions will help to structure the activity:

- What did you do?
- What happened then?
- Were there any disagreements?
- What did you agree about?
- Were there any difficult moments?
- Were there any funny moments?
- What was the first idea?
- How did this idea change as you worked together on it?

Using our skills

Here the members of the QC take time to share their own experience of using specific QC techniques. Useful questions include:

- How well did you use the new methods which we have learned (e.g. Forcefield Analysis, Why? Why?, How? How?)?
- How useful were they?
- How productive were they?
- Did everyone have a chance to practise the skill?

Working together

Again open-ended questions enable QC members to review their own strengths and weaknesses as a team:

- What did we each do to help other members of the group?
- In how many different ways did we communicate with one another?
- Could we have worked differently with one another?

Developing a vocabulary of feelings

It is very important for QC members to develop a vocabulary which accurately captures and expresses pupils' feelings as they engaged in the QC process. The following words can be used as the basis for discussion – or (better still!) the QC itself can brainstorm its own list. Each member in turn says 'Today I felt . . . in the QC' and selects a word from the list to complete the sentence. You can encourage other members to reply with their own perceptions of that person – 'Today in the QC you looked . . .' – by inserting a word from the list to complete the sentence. Any differences of perspective can then be explored.

angry	positive	isolated	accepting
open	supportive	creative	inspiring
friendly	patient	hurt	upset
puzzled	left out	gentle	sympathetic
co-operative	lonely	frustrated	appreciated
sensitive	involved	warm	sad
cold	happy	uncertain	disappointed

Using video

Videotape the QC at work. You can view the video either with the QC or make it a whole-class activity in which all QCs take part. Ask members of the group on the video to press the pause button at any point which is of significance to them. You can use open-ended questions to explore the processes of the group:

* What was happening at that moment?
* What were you feeling then?
* Are there any things which you would have liked to say at that point?
* What got in the way?

One-word circle

At the end of an activity, members of the QC form a circle and give a one-word summary of their feelings about the activity.

Diaries

Pupils can derive benefit from keeping diaries in which they record:
* new ideas, concepts, information they learned in the QC;
* what they learned about their own ability to discuss, agree and express ideas;

- their own contribution to the group process;
- how they saw the group as a whole.

Telegrams

Members of the QC send a telegram to the group in which they write briefly about their view of the activity.

> I feel that this session....
>
> ....
>
> ....
>
> ....
>
> ....
>
> ....
>
> ....
>
> ....

From these explorations of bullying behaviour, all pupils can gain a better under-standing of the problem; they can examine their own behaviour and attitudes; they can rehearse effective ways of standing up to bullying behaviour. Teachers can aim to empower pupils to take action against bullying and give them a chance to practise the strategies and vocabulary which will help them to do this.

Using drama to explore personal experiences

Drama is an important medium for enabling young people to become more socially aware. The skills of empathy and the capacity to understand another person's perspective can be enhanced through the opportunity to explore situations within the safety of role-play. Drama is also an effective way for pupils to explore the emotions which are aroused by disturbing experiences such as being victimised or being a witness to someone else's humiliation. In this chapter we shall present some examples of drama activities which can help pupils share and reflect on personal experiences of being bullied or of being a bystander while bullying takes place.

Using drama to explore the motivation to bully

The use of drama gives participants the opportunity to identify with different characters and enables them to enter into another person's experience through sympathetic re-enactment. In order to understand the phenomenon of bullying more fully, it is also necessary to have some insights into what motivates people to engage in bullying behaviour. Do some social contexts actually encourage bullying, e.g. hierarchical organisations where power is often misused and where it is difficult for victims to complain without further humiliation? Do some individuals 'invite' bullying through their provocative behaviour? Are some children who bully being victimised elsewhere?

ACTIVITY BOX 4.13   BEING BULLIED

Think about a time when you have been hurt by someone calling you names, leaving you out or making you do things you don't want to do. How did you feel when this was happening?

Individually make up a monologue (this is when only one person speaks). Explain what happened and how you felt.

You have come home from school and you are alone in your bedroom. In front of your mirror you run through the scene again. You say the things you didn't dare say at the time. Either prepare this scene on your own to share with the class or work with a partner with your partner playing your reflection in the mirror.

In a group take it in turns to tell your bullying stories. As a group decide on one and make it into a short play to show to the rest of the class. Include at least two 'insights' into how the bullied pupil is feeling. You could do this by 'freezing' the action and talking directly to the audience or you could include it in the dialogue.

Think about the kinds of things people do with their bodies and faces during a bullying situation. How do they stand? What sorts of things do they do with their hands and faces? Mime your bullying scene, emphasising the posture and gestures of the pupils involved.

Share your bullying stories. Think about what you actually did in the situation and devise two alternative resolutions to the situations. Enact them. Which is the most effective? Why?

Discussion points

• How does it feel to be bullied?
• What are the consequences of being bullied?
• What should you do if you are bullied?

ACTIVITY BOX 4.14   BEING A BYSTANDER

Have you ever known that someone is being bullied but not done anything about it?

- In groups of 4/5, share your stories. How did you feel? Were you comfortable or uncomfortable?
- In pairs, one person take on the role of the bullied pupil; the other take on the role of the bystander who did not help. Bystanders try to explain why you did not help; what dilemmas did you face?
- Re-enact the bullying scene, but this time intervene. How did you feel? How effective were you?

Discussion points

- How does it feel to be a bystander?
- Are inactive bystanders as bad as the bully?
- How do bystanders make the bullying worse?
- What can bystanders do to help the bullied pupil?

Are some pupils who bully modelling themselves on domineering adults or older siblings? Are we all capable of bullying in certain circumstances? Can any of us say in all honesty, 'I have never bullied'? The following activities provide ideas for exploring this aspect of the subject of bullying. (See **Activity Boxes 4.13, 4.14, 4.15** and **4.16**.)

Role cards with background information about contrasting characters can give pupils a framework within which to explore different facets of bullying. **Activity Box 4.17** illustrates the potential for bullying behaviour in the context of social interaction at a party. To heighten the drama, the situation here concerns access to a rare but expensive drug which could save the life of a child. The enactment of the three roles – doctor, scientist and parent – raises challenging moral dilemmas. Discussion points could include:

- Is bullying ever justifiable?
- How do people get drawn into bullying others?
- How do pupils who bully get their power?
- What are alternatives to bullying?

This activity may even make it possible for participants in the drama to reflect on their own potential for using aggressive methods in order to get their own way.

ACTIVITY BOX 4.15   BULLYING OTHERS

Have you ever bullied anyone? A younger sister or brother; a new pupil; a younger child or someone in your class? Think about what you did and what led you to do this. How did you feel when you were bullying someone?

• In a group of 3/4 share your stories.
• Make a list of reasons for bullying – are there any good reasons for bullying someone?
• Try to think of the things that might have stopped you from bullying; improvise some short scenes which demonstrate how you could have been stopped. Which are the most effective? Why?

Discussion points

• How does it feel to bully someone?
• What are the alternatives to bullying?
• What are the consequences of bullying others?

.ACTIVITY BOX 4.16   WHAT MAKES PEOPLE BULLY?

In threes, one of you has a precious object. Decide what it is. The other person tries to get the precious object off the other. You have two minutes. After two minutes, swap over. The third person is an observer. Note what kinds of tactics are used to try and get the object. Which are aggressive, manipulative, threatening etc.?

As a whole group discuss how you felt when you were using/on the receiving end of these attempts to get the object. Were any methods more reasonable than others? Were any bullying?

Put an empty chair in the centre of the group. Imagine that someone is sitting on the chair – the person sitting there has often been involved in bullying others. Build up a description of the person – age, gender, physical characteristics, personality, childhood, friends, family background, interests, strengths and weaknesses. Why does this person bully others? When did she or he start? Has she/he ever been bullied?

ACTIVITY BOX 4.17   IS IT EVER RIGHT TO BULLY?

Working in groups of three, each pupil receives a role card:

The doctor

You are a doctor in a hospital. You have a patient who will die unless they receive a particular drug. The patient is the son of a very close friend of yours. The drug is very expensive and the hospital can't afford to buy it. However, you have another friend who works for the company which makes the drug. You want her/him to either let you have a sample or to reduce the price so that you can buy it. You know that her/his daughter is on the waiting list for an ear operation and it is likely to be another eight months before the operation is carried out. You could do it sooner. You meet this friend at a party.

The scientist

You work for a drug company which produces a wonder drug which can cure many rare diseases. It is very expensive. Last month, a colleague of yours was sacked because they undercharged a hospital for the drug. You personally think it is unfair to charge so much for the drug but your boss won't listen to you. You also know that the drug has very nasty side effects and isn't always totally effective. You are at a party and a friend approaches you to talk about the drug.

The parent

You are the parent of a child who has a rare disease. It can only be cured by a particular drug and the drug is too expensive for you, or the hospital to buy. You visit your son every day and just watch him slowly dying. You are at a party and you see the doctor who is treating your son. You approach her/him. She/he is talking to another person. You realise that this other person works for the drug company who make the drug which will save your son.

Improvise the scene at the party. Did any of the three resort to bullying tactics during the conversation? Was it justifiable to resort to bullying at any point? Was it morally right? Was it effective?

Using drama to explore the consequences of bullying

In the short term, bullying can be a very effective means of getting your own way, but there are longer-term consequences for the pupils who are directly involved and for those who observe it happening. It is important to explore these outcomes and to consider what the cost of bullying is. **Activity Box 4.18** gives pupils the opportunity to reflect on the impact which bullying has on relationships within the peer group. It also offers the hope that people can change. Discussion points could include the following:

- How does bullying affect people immediately (emotionally, physically, psycho-logically)?
- What are the long-term consequences of bullying?
- 'Once a bully, always a bully; once a victim always a victim.' How true is this statement?

ACTIVITY BOX 4.18

In threes, improvise the following situation:

Two of you are sitting on a park bench. You are in your mid-30s and have known each other since you were at school. Another person approaches and sits down to eat her/his sandwiches. One of you recognises the third person – she/he too used to go to your school. She/he made your lives miserable and used to bully you all the time. One of you changed schools to try to stop it happening. The third person recognises you and starts to talk about your school days. Through the conversation explore how the bullying affected you all when you were at school and how it has affected your lives since. How do you feel about each other now?

Activity Boxes 4.19, 4.20 and 4.21 show the consequences of bullying as it affects families, teachers and peers.

Getting out of role

When children or adults have been involved in role-plays where they have taken on the role of a bullied pupil, bystander or bullying pupil, it is important to spend some time bringing them out of the role. This can be done by asking each person to say their real name and something about themselves.

ACTIVITY BOX 4.19   HOW DOES BULLYING AFFECT FAMILIES?

- You have been caught bullying someone at school. Your parents have been contacted by the school to tell them what has been happening. You are standing outside the front door with the key in your hand. What are you feeling/thinking? You enter the house. Your family are sitting around the table . . .

Improvise the rest of the scene. Explore how different members of your family feel about your bullying behaviour; how do their reactions and feelings affect the bullying pupil?

- In the Doctor's waiting room, a parent of the bullying person is sitting opposite the parent of the bullied child. There is nobody else in the waiting room. Improvise the conversation – try to reach a peaceful outcome.

- Imagine you are the family of a bullied pupil. As yet, you don't know that she/he is being bullied but she/he has been acting strangely for a long time – coming home in a bad mood, with unexplained cuts and bruises, not wanting to go to school in the morning. Now money has started to go missing, you suspect your daughter/son has been stealing. You decide to confront her/him this evening. Improvise the scene. When you find out that she/he has been bullied, how do you react? What do you advise her/him to do?

Discussion points
- How can families help pupils who are involved in bullying?
- How soon should schools involve families when there is a bullying incident?

Other resources

There are a number of plays and videos available which are about bullying. These can be used to stimulate role play and discussion. Pupils can explore the characters in the plays and their motivation; they can devise alternative endings or can begin to construct their own interpretations of the play.

Taking drama to a wider audience

The improvised work which pupils can develop through drama can be used as a basis for performances for other pupils and for families. Actually setting pupils the task of

ACTIVITY BOX 4.20   HOW DO TEACHERS FEEL ABOUT BULLYING?

- A member of staff is confronted by two pupils. Both are very convincing – one says that she/he is being bullied by the other; the other denies this. Improvise the scene.

- In the staffroom, one teacher is talking to two others. She/he is very worried about a pupil in her/his class. She/he suspects the pupil is being bullied but has no evidence. What do the other teachers advise her/him to do?

- A teacher keeps on picking on one pupil in her/his class. She/he calls the pupil nasty names. She/he quite often tells the pupil off for no reason and embarrasses her/him if she/he doesn't know what to do. Improvise a scene where the pupil and a group of friends are talking about what she/he should do to resolve the situation.

Discussion points
- What can teachers do about bullying?
- What should pupils do if they think they are being bullied by a teacher?
- Sometimes groups of pupils pick on teachers – what can schools do about this?

developing a play or workshop for a specified audience can be motivating for them and helpful in communicating the school's anti-bullying values. Audiences can be found amongst the school population, in the community and in feeder schools. Local Theatre in Education groups may also have devised material relating to the theme of bullying.

Literature as a stimulus for discussion and creative writing about bullying issues

Literature is a powerful medium for capturing experiences and emotions which, when used with sensitivity and imagination, can retain its appeal to young people through-out the school years. There are many novels and poems which address the issue of bullying behaviour in a thought-provoking way. For primary schools, stories such as *The Diddakoi* by Rumer Godden; *The present takers* by Aidan Chambers or *The Heartstone Odyssey* by Arvan Kumar demonstrate the unfairness of bullying behaviour and introduce anti-bullying strategies tried out by the characters. *The Heartstone Odyssey* is also useful as a way of raising issues of racial harassment. It is backed by an

ACTIVITY BOX 4.21   WHAT IS THE IMPACT ON THE BYSTANDERS?

In groups of 4/5, each group receives one situation card. They role-play the scene described.

- At home, your older brother wants you to do his homework for him as he wants to go out with his mates. You are better at maths than he is. When you say, 'No, I am meeting some friends', he threatens to tell your parents that you got into trouble at school the week before. They will be angry if they find out.

- In the corridor, a group of pupils crowd round another pupil. They won't let her/him pass. They begin to push her/him around and call her/him names.

- In the playground, three pupils are waiting by the school gate. As the younger pupils enter the school, they grab one and demand some dinner money.

- In the classroom, one pupil snatches the bag off another. They empty it onto a desk and begin to rip up her/his English homework book.

- In the playground, a pupil comes up to join in a game of football. One other pupil won't let her/him play.

Each small group presents their drama situation to the whole group. The audience are all bystanders. They can intervene in the role-play whenever they want. What can they do? How can they help?

- Three friends are discussing a bullied pupil in their class. They don't like seeing this person being bullied but aren't sure what they should do. One of the friends thinks that if they intervene, they will make it worse and probably the bullying pupils will turn on them. The other friend thinks that they should stand up for the bullied person the next time it happens. The third person is not sure which is best. Improvise their conversation.

Discussion points

- How can bystanders stop bullying?
- Is there a right way and a wrong way to intervene in a bullying situation?
- What are the dilemmas faced by a bystander?

INFORMATION BOX 4.4 RESOURCES AVAILABLE

For junior schools **The trouble with Tom** produced by Central TV and screened as part of their Social Development series, tells the story of an 'odd boy out', Tom. He is ostracised by his peers and bullied by a gang of boys in his class. The situation comes to a head on a residential camp. The video comes with teachers' notes.

It's no' just rough 'n' tumble is produced by the South Edinburgh Crime Prevention Panel. A primary school pupil, Kelly, is bullied by a gang of boys. She is helped by a dream, where a 'Warrior of Rap' helps her to devise self-defence strategies. The video comes with an information pack, musical cassette and ideas for drama.

For secondary schools **Sticks and stones** presents a series of short dramatisations and personal accounts from the perspective of the bullied pupil, the bullying pupil and the bystander. The accompanying information pack includes a reading list, two short role-plays and a checklist of anti-bullying strategies.

'Only playing, Miss' is a script and video about a young schoolboy who is tormented by another pupil following his father's death. The play shows how bullying can be stopped and offers insight into the difficulties faced by both bully and victim. The script contains a section on drama ideas. These materials have also been used with younger pupils.

The terrible fate of Humpty Dumpty is a short play about a young boy who is called names and tormented by a group of peers. The bullying builds to a crescendo and finally results in the boy's death.

---

organisation which promotes 'story circles', regular meetings which deliberately set a forum for discussion of themes in the story and personal experiences of bullying.

Some stories for secondary-aged pupils – for example *The chocolate war* by Robert Cormier, *Lord of the flies* by William Golding, *The friends* by Rosa Guy – go further in their exploration of the abuse of power which underlies bullying behaviour. Stories like *My mate Shofiq* by Jan Needle and *Roll of thunder, hear my cry* by Mildred Taylor address the issue of racially motivated bullying and harassment.

Literature and creative writing, like drama, offer young people the opportunity to develop a sense of themselves in different contexts and to experience new perspectives on how to relate to other people. Through their reading, writing and discussion about themes of personal and social concern, pupils can heighten their emotional responsiveness to the problem of bullying. They can learn more about the nature of the problem; they can identify motivation to bully within the characters; they can understand the immediate and far-reaching consequences of bullying behaviour; they can grapple with the social dilemmas and emotional turmoil that face most people who encounter bullying behaviour.

Pupils write differently for different audiences. This is relevant when we consider the power of writing to change perspectives on an issue such as bullying. By creating opportunities to read literature, discuss passages of text and write in different modes for a range of audiences, you can contribute significantly to the creation of a climate of openness and trust in the school – the kind of climate where bullying is less likely to flourish. What pupils write and how they respond to literature depends greatly on the ways in which teachers ask questions and on the sensitivity with which responses can be thoughtfully explored within peer groups.

The next section presents some ideas for discussion-based and creative writing activities which can be used with a text or independently. The activities demonstrate ideas for encouraging pupils to think carefully about the implications of bullying behaviour and to develop greater empathy with the children who are involved in bullying situations. The extract which we have chosen as illustration is taken from *The Heartstone Odyssey* (Kumar, 1985) but clearly teachers will use their judgement in selecting appropriate texts to stimulate creative writing and discussion on the theme of bullying.

Personal and imaginative accounts

Here the teacher can use a piece of text which addresses the issue of bullying and so create a framework within which the pupils can discuss what is happening, why it is happening, how effectively different characters respond to the situation and how it relates to their own experience (see **Activity Box 4.22**).

The process of sharing responses to literature on a sensitive issue m .y create a climate of trust in the class which can facilitate imaginative writing on the part of the pupils about their own experiences of bullying. **Activity Box 4.23** gives some further ideas.

Inquiring and information-giving

An important aspect of understanding a controversial issue like bullying is the possession of accurate, reliable information on the subject (see also **Activity Boxes 4.5, 4.6, 4.7**). Pupils benefit from opportunities to develop skills in gathering information and in interpreting their findings. There are also skills to be learned in the

ACTIVITY BOX 4.22   RESPONSE TO FICTION

One of the men reached up and grabbed the inspector's jacket, pulling him down. 'I told you Paki, we don't take orders from your kind.' . . . Snuggletoes (the youngest mouse) could stand it no longer. Perhaps he hadn't been on adventures before, but he wasn't going to sit and watch this. With one jump he was off the table, across the carriage, and beside the old lady. 'Can I borrow one of your pencils please?' he said. 'Of course,' whispered the old lady, 'but be careful.' 'No', said Snuggletoes, he'd seen enough of being careful . . . Snuggletoes took a big scoop of ice cream from the tub and balanced a spoon across the pencil like a seesaw. Then he climbed on to the edge of the tub and jumped down, stamping on the spoon as he landed. The ice cream flew through the air and hit the man straight in the face. He jumped back in surprise and let go of the ticket inspector . . . 'Vermin, I'll get you for that and your Paki friends.' The two men got up and began to lurch down the carriage. (Kumar, 1985)

Discuss what this extract tells you about Snuggletoes.
Interview Snuggletoes in one of the following ways:

- The teacher adopts the role of Snuggletoes. The class questions him about himself (in role) and his life.
- A student teacher or visitor takes on the role of Snuggletoes and is questioned by the class.
- The pupils divide into groups of 4/5. Ask one pupil to take on the role of Snuggletoes and be interviewed.

Ask the class to write down their own feelings about the episode.
Encourage them to write a letter from Snuggletoes in which he describes what happened to him that day.
Enact the scene. What does it feel like to be:

- Snuggletoes
- the old lady
- the inspector
- one of the two men?

ACTIVITY BOX 4.23 STANDING BACK FROM YOUR OWN EXPERIENCE

Think about a time when you have been hurt by someone calling you names, leaving you out or making you do things you don't want to do. Write a poem or short story describing what happened and how you felt.

Thinking about your own experiences of bullying, as someone directly involved or as a bystander, draw a series of pictures which shows a bullying incident unfolding. Try to show what is happening and how the people involved are feeling.

In a group of 4 or 5 people, share your bullying stories. Discuss the kinds of things you could have done to avoid or stop the situation. What sorts of things should you do after you have been bullied? Prepare an advice pamphlet for other children who are being bullied.

Write a story about the leader of a bullying gang. You could either write it as if you were this person, giving her or his view of school and home or you could write it from the point of view of someone who knows her/him – either as an observer, a teacher, parent, friend or victim.

Imagine you are being bullied by someone in your school. Write some entries in your diary. You could include your thoughts on other aspects of school as well as the bullying incidents.

In pairs, imagine that one of you is friends with someone who keeps on picking on a girl in your class and the other is a friend or older sister/brother. You are worried about your friend's behaviour but are afraid to challenge her/him about it. What advice can the other person offer? Write a script of their conversation.

communication of this information in accessible and stimulating ways. The following activities outline some of the techniques which pupils can learn in the gathering of evidence, its interpretation and its dissemination (**Activity Boxes 4.24** and **4.25**).

Debate

Once the evidence is gathered in, there is a basis for informed discussion and debate. In order to debate an issue from different perspectives, pupils need practice in marshalling arguments. They can deepen their understanding if they really listen to a range of points of view and hear the reasons for them. The following activities aim

ACTIVITY BOX 4.24   INVESTIGATING HOW BULLYING AFFECTS YOUNG PEOPLE

Design and implement a questionnaire to find out how many pupils in your year group have been bullied. How did it make them feel? Analyse the results and present them as a report to the headteacher.

Bullying doesn't just take place in your school. Talk to your friends and relatives and try to collect together stories about bullying experiences. Write a short newspaper article entitled 'Bullying – a problem for all of us' based on the stories you hear.

Find out ten facts about bullying. Present them in a leaflet for younger pupils.

ACTIVITY BOX 4.25   DISSEMINATING INFORMATION

Designing a special issue on bullying

You run a young people's magazine. You are very concerned about bullying and you decide to print a special edition about bullying and ways of stopping it. Your magazine should include some of the following:

- stories about bullying
- interviews with pupils who bully, bullied pupils, witnesses, families or staff, etc.
- photo-stories
- cartoons
- fact file features, e.g. 20 facts about bullying; 10 ways to stop bullying
- bullying survey results, e.g. how many people in your year have bullied someone/been bullied?
- letters to the editor
- advice page
- questionnaire
- book review

Producing a documentary

Make your own radio or TV documentary about bullying. It could include a short play about bullying as well as interviews with pupils, parents and teachers. Try to keep it to 30 minutes in length. Decide who your audience will be before you begin to script it.

Spearheading an anti-bullying campaign

The government is worried about bullying and wants to reduce the amount of bullying in schools. You are an advertising consultancy whom they have approached to design a campaign to raise awareness about the problems of bullying in schools and to try to encourage people to do something about it. In groups of four or five discuss your ideas for this campaign. You could produce pamphlets, posters, badges and TV/radio commercial slots. You will need a slogan, a logo and possibly a catchy jingle if your campaign is going to go on air. Decide who your audience will be – ideally you will produce materials which could be used around schools as well as distributed to families and the wider community.

Guidelines

In pairs or threes, write some guidelines for people in the school telling them what they should do if they see someone bullying anyone. You may need different guidelines for different people, i.e. pupils, teachers, supervisors, families, etc. Design a poster to present them.

to give pupils the opportunity to experience at first hand the implicit values and assumptions which underlie many everyday opinions.

Activities like these (**Activity Boxes 4.26** and **4.27**) may also give pupils the opportunity to express their ideas on how to resolve the problem of bullying in their own school environment. Some of the techniques from the Quality Circle method can be adapted for follow-up lessons stimulated by the pupils' responses.

SUMMARY

In this chapter we have offered a few ideas for tackling bullying through the curriculum. We are sure you will be able to think of many more. Through the curriculum you can offer all pupils the opportunity to explore the issue of bullying. They can learn to understand the problem and begin to examine their own attitudes and behaviour towards their peers. Furthermore, through the

ACTIVITY BOX 4.26   DEBATING AN ISSUE

'Sticks and stones will break my bones but words will never hurt me.' How true is this old rhyme? In your group make a list of all the kinds of bullying you can think of. Which are the most hurtful and which are the most harmful?

'Pupils who are found bullying others will be immediately excluded.' How effective is exclusion when dealing with bullying? Does it change the behaviour of the pupil involved? How should schools respond to bullying behaviour? Interview some other people around school as well as people outside school to find out how others feel about exclusion. Put your findings into a short essay which argues the case for or against exclusion.

ACTIVITY BOX 4.27   PRACTICAL STRATEGIES FOR TACKLING BULLYING

Think about bullying in your school. What sort of things help to support bullying? For example teachers who don't like you to 'tell tales'; no supervisors in a particular part of the school; believing it's 'cool' to ignore people who are unhappy, etc. Make a list of all the things you can think of which might help pupils who bully to carry on their victimisation of other pupils. When you have done this, consider each one and try to think of ways of changing it. Try to think of things that teachers, pupils and other staff could do which would make it difficult for bullying to take place.

How can bullying affect young people? Sometimes pupils who are being bullied are afraid to tell anyone what is happening to them. What sorts of signs can parents and teachers watch out for in children who might be being bullied? If you become aware of someone behaving in this way what can you do to help them?

What can schools do to help victims of bullying? In small groups discuss things which might help victims to cope with the hurt that bullying causes as well as to learn ways of stopping it happening again. Try to make a list of ten ideas – you could include some things which pupils could do and some things which the teachers could do.

curriculum you can approach the problem of bullying participatively with your pupils therefore providing them with the opportunity to develop, practise and implement their own solutions. In this way we can foster a greater sense of community and introduce our pupils to the skills of citizenship.

F·I·V·E | # how to respond to bullying behaviour

SONIA SHARP
HELEN COWIE
PETER K. SMITH

In addition to promoting an anti-bullying ethos as a preventative measure against bullying, schools need methods for responding directly to bullying incidents.

Mild sanctions can be useful in responding to one-off incidents of bullying which do not result in actual physical harm. A reprimand may be sufficient to deter a pupil from continuing with name-calling or mild teasing.

Any pupil who is persistently involved in bullying behaviour despite the repeated intervention of the school, probably needs help and firm guidance. There will be a very small number of pupils who do not respond to the usual range of responses and strategies available to schools. Expert assistance may be needed in planning ways of working with these pupils.

However serious, any response to incidents of bullying should:

- be clear, honest and direct, avoiding the use of humiliation, sarcasm, aggression, threat or manipulation;
- be immediate, with possible follow-up in the longer term;
- involve recording what has happened, who was involved and what action was taken;
- involve the family at an early stage;
- provide opportunities for the pupils to discuss with one another ways of resolving the problem.

In this chapter we will describe some strategies specifically designed to help pupils who are involved in bullying situations. The first, the Method of Shared Concern, aims to change the behaviour of the bullying pupils; the second, Assertiveness Training, aims to teach bullied pupils how to resist bullying attempts.

The Method of Shared Concern

The Method of Shared Concern is a counselling-based approach for resolving bullying situations. It was first devised by Anatol Pikas, a Swedish psychologist based in the Education Department at Uppsala University. In the UK a similar method for working with bullying pupils has since been developed called the No Blame Approach (Maines and Robinson, 1992). Both of these methods have one common factor: they concentrate on finding a solution to the problem.

The Method of Shared Concern is particularly appropriate for bullying situations where a group of pupils have been bullying one or more pupils on a regular basis for some time. It is only considered appropriate for pupils aged 9 years and upward, although we know of schools that have used this method successfully with younger pupils.

The overall aim of the method is to establish ground rules which will enable the pupils to coexist within the same school. It does not aim to create a friendship between the pupils or to uncover the details of the bullying situation. The teacher uses a specific script to manoeuvre the bullying pupils into changing their behaviour.

The Method of Shared Concern starts from the premise that there is a problem – it is fact that the bullied pupil is unhappy in school. Individual discussion with each of the pupils involved in the bullying situation establishes that there is cause for concern regarding this pupil. The teacher deliberately avoids becoming entangled in fact-finding or apportioning blame. All that is needed is agreement that the child being bullied is 'having a bad time'.

The method has three stages:

- individual 'chats' with each pupil involved (about 7 to 10 minutes per child);
- follow-up interviews with each pupil (about 3 minutes per child);
- group meeting (about half an hour).

The time span between each stage is typically one week. In practice, the actual length of time depends on the availability of the teacher, although these intervals should always be less than two weeks.

We recommend that this method is used as part of the graded disciplinary procedure set out by the school's anti-bullying policy. Teachers need to know when to use this method and what alternative action to take if it does not work. This implies that there must be a follow-up system which will establish whether or not the bullying has stopped.

Stage 1 First meetings

The first interview with each pupil must be the most carefully structured. Pikas has devised a script for teachers to follow. We have found that the success of the method depends on teachers adhering to this script, which is described later in this section.

Sequence

The sequence of interviews is important. Bullying situations often involve more than two pupils. Although only one person may actually have directly done or said nasty things, she or he will often be supported, backed up or even encouraged by one or more of her/his peers. The teacher will meet with all of these pupils, in turn, beginning with the 'ringleader'. The ringleader may not be the person who actually carried out the bullying – some ringleaders take a directional role. The ringleader is the person who seems to hold the most power within the group. The victim is interviewed last.

There are two reasons for this order. First, as the method is non-confrontational, the pupils return to their class relaxed. This is communicated non-verbally to the other pupils involved in the bullying situation. If they observe that their 'leader' is not tense on return, they are more likely to be positive about the interview and consequently, more likely to be co-operative. The bullying pupils are interviewed before the victim to avoid any accusations of 'telling tales'.

Preliminaries

Before starting the interviews, talk to the class teacher and/or other adults who have seen any bullying. Get what information you can (e.g. Who is likely ringleader? Is the bullied pupil provocative?). Make sure there is a suitable place for the interviews, and book in times to see the pupils concerned with the class teachers. Ask the class teachers *not* to forewarn the pupils. At the appointed time, they should simply send them to see you.

Timing

The first interviews should take place consecutively and without a break. It should be possible to see a whole bullying group in the space of one lesson. With exceptionally large groups, i.e. more than eight pupils, it will be important to select a time which will be sufficiently long, e.g. when an assembly precedes a lesson. Try to avoid interviewing some of the group before a break and some after. If possible, there should be as little opportunity for the pupils to talk with one another during the first interview stage.

Location

The meetings should take place in a room which will be undisturbed and offer some privacy – e.g. an empty classroom or office (without a telephone!). The pupil and teacher always sit down for these interviews. Care should be taken about the seating arrangements. Try to choose chairs of equal height; if this is not possible, then the teacher should sit on the lower seat. The chairs should not be at a desk, and should be at a slight angle. If there is a window which looks on to the corridor or an area where other pupils might be passing by, sit the pupil with her or his back to it.

Attitude

Sometimes bullying behaviour can provoke very strong feelings in adults. The teacher must be able to maintain a non-judgemental and neutral attitude towards the bullying pupils. If she or he feels angry or punitive towards the pupil then this method should not be used.

The nature of the pupil–teacher relationship does not seem to affect the method. Schools should use their own discretion concerning who uses this method with the pupils. It is important, however, that the same teacher is involved in all three stages.

Learning the method

We advise that teachers are trained to use this script. It only consists of four essential lines, but our experience is that it is quite difficult for adults to keep to using them without practice. As teachers, we tend to talk too much and ask too many interrogational questions, quite often without even realising what we are doing. It is hard not to slip back into our usual ways of talking with pupils. If you want to use this method, find someone with experience of it who can offer you training or spend time rehearsing carefully through role-play, with an observer providing feedback, before using the method with pupils. The method does work *if you stick to the script*! When you are role-playing with other teachers, remember that the objective of the rehearsal is to learn and practise the script. It is not helpful if the teacher playing the part of the bullying pupil is deliberately obstructive in an unrealistic way.

Script for bullying pupils

So, you are expecting your first pupil (the ringleader). Make sure you feel relaxed. When the pupil enters, ask her or him to sit down. Look at her or him, then wait until the pupil looks at you. A glance is enough. Then start.

The essential lines are:

1 *I hear you have been nasty to X. Tell me about it.* (Follow up denial with: *Yes, but nasty things have been happening to X. Tell me about it.*)

   Now listen to what the pupil tells you. Don't be worried by long silences – give the pupil time to think. Don't accuse or blame. Try to avoid asking questions. Be accepting if the pupil feels justified in their behaviour towards the other pupil – they may feel quite angry towards him or her. Work towards an understanding that X is having a bad time (whoever is to blame).

2 *So, it sounds like X is having a bad time in school.* Said with force and emphasis. By now, the pupil should assent to this. Move quickly on to say:

3 *OK. I was wondering what you could do to help X in this situation.* See what solution the pupil can come up with. Be encouraging. When some practical and relevant step forward is forthcoming, say:

4 *Excellent. You try that out for a week and we will meet and see how you have got on. Goodbye.*

You then repeat this script with each pupil in turn. **Information Box 5.1** offers an example of the script in practice.

There are variations to the script for possible problem situations, e.g. the pupil who refuses to talk; the pupil who tries to bargain; the pupil who will not co-operate. These are described below. If, however, the teacher feels that the interview is going wrong, the best thing to do is stop it. Simply say: 'OK. I think we'll leave it there for today. I will see you again on . . .'. However, we have found that pupils are usually very co-operative *as long as the teacher is not accusatory and sticks to the script.*

Possible problems

No ideas for solutions

First of all, allow the pupil time to think. Don't be afraid of silence. If they really cannot think of a solution you can offer a suggestion but always gain the pupil's permission first. Say 'I have an idea. Would you like to hear it?'

The unco-operative child

Do not try to encourage a silent or unco-operative pupil to respond. Simply wait in

INFORMATION BOX 5.1 AN INTERVIEW WITH A BULLYING PUPIL

Teacher	I hear you have been nasty to Matthew.
Pupil	No, it wasn't me.
Teacher	Nasty things have been happening to Matthew. Tell me about it. (*Long silence . . .*)
Pupil	Well, it's the others not me.
Teacher	Mmm.
Pupil	They've just been getting at him. He asks for it. (*Silence*)
Pupil	It started last term. Matthew was showing off about going on holiday. He'd bought a bag back, so we . . . they hid it in the cupboard. He went mad and we started chucking it round the room and it went out the window. Now he gets his bag messed around with sometimes . . . he gets called bag boy . . . it's only a laugh . . . he just doesn't fit in.
Teacher	So, it sounds as if Matthew has been having a bad time in school.
Pupil	Well, I suppose so.
Teacher	OK. I was wondering what you could do to help him in this situation.
Pupil	Me?
Teacher	Yes, you. (*Silence*)
Pupil	Well . . . I don't know really . . . I suppose I could tell the others to leave him alone.
Teacher	Excellent! Good. You try that out for a week and we will meet at this time, here on Tuesday and see how you have got on. Goodbye.
Pupil	Is that all?

silence for them to speak. If after a few minutes they have not said anything, say, 'It seems that you don't want to talk today. You'd better go back to your class now.' They may well begin to talk at this point!

An impractical solution

If a pupil offers an impractical or ridiculous solution, do not reject it negatively. Ask, 'So, if this were to happen, the bullying would stop?'

INFORMATION BOX 5.2   INTERVIEW WITH THE BULLIED PUPIL

Teacher   Hello, Matthew. Sit down. I want to talk with you because I hear some nasty things have been happening to you.

Matthew   Yes. It's the others in my class. They just keep on picking on me. They won't leave me alone. They mess around with my bag . . . putting muck in it and things like that.

Teacher   You sound as if you're fed up with it.

Matthew   It just doesn't stop. The rest of the class join in now.

Teacher   Is there anything you can think of which might help the situation?

Matthew   I could change schools.

Teacher   Mmm. So you feel it would be better to get out of the situation altogether?

Matthew   Well, sometimes. But I don't suppose my mum would let me. They're not so bad when I hang around with Simon.

Teacher   So being with someone helps the situation?

Matthew   Yes. He backs me up when I tell them to stop it.

Teacher   So he supports you?

Matthew   Yes. I could sit next to him.

Teacher   OK. You do that over the next week and then we'll have another chat to see how things have been going. OK? 'Bye then.

A solution that depends on someone else's action

Don't bargain. Say, 'I was thinking more about something you could do yourself.'

Continual complaints about the provocative behaviour of the bullied pupil

Pupils often feel very justified in their bullying behaviour. They perceive that the bullied pupil 'asked for it' in some way. Don't reject the pupil's anger or frustration against the bullied pupil; accept their feelings but still maintain that the bullied pupil is having 'a bad time in school'.

Script for bullied pupils

For the bullied pupils, the script is less structured. However, you do have to try and find out whether the pupil is, as Pikas would say, a 'classic victim' (not responsible for their being bullied) or a 'provocative victim' (a pupil who contributes to their being bullied by provoking others in some way). For the 'classic victim' the role is primarily one of support. See **Information Box 5.2**.

With the bullied pupil you adopt a counselling role, although still helping her or him to find ways in which they too can be active in improving the situation. You may find it helpful to add to this interview by rehearsing assertive strategies with the bullied pupil.

If the pupil is a 'provocative bullied pupil', you should also try and help the pupil realise that their own behaviour is contributing to the situation and that they too must change. See **Information Box 5.3** for an example.

Outcomes

As a result of these first interviews, each pupil suggests how they could change their behaviour in some small way. The most common suggestions are: leaving the bullied

---

INFORMATION BOX 5.3   INTERVIEW WITH THE BULLIED PUPIL WHO IS PROVOCATIVE

Teacher   Hello, Matthew. Sit down. I want to talk with you because I hear some nasty things have been happening to you.

Matthew   Yes. It's the others in my class. They just keep on picking on me. They won't leave me alone. They mess around with my bag . . . putting muck in it and things like that.

Teacher   You sound as if you're fed up with it.

Matthew   It just doesn't stop. The rest of the class join in now.

Teacher   Tell me more about what happens. How does it all start?

Matthew   It's usually when I go over and sit by them. They just can't take a joke.

Teacher   So you play jokes on them?

Matthew   Yes, just messing around. I go on really good holidays and they never do so I ask them where they are going . . . it makes them really mad. They're just jealous.

Teacher   Then they get cross with you. What happens when they get cross with you?

Matthew   Well, that's when they started messing around with my bag.

Teacher   Is there anything you can think of which might help the situation?

Matthew   I could leave them alone, I suppose.

Teacher   OK. You do that over the next week and then we'll have another chat to see how things have been going. OK? 'Bye then.

pupil alone; sticking up for the bullied pupil; being friendly towards the bullied pupil. The interviews finish with each pupil agreeing to try to achieve their suggestion for the following week.

Age and gender differences

Younger primary age pupils cannot always suggest ways for improving the situation. They may need the teacher to take a more directive role.

Girls seem to find it harder to perceive a middle ground between 'best friends' and 'enemies'. We have found that it is wise to point out to girls that the kinds of solutions we are looking for in this method do not *have* to involve becoming close friends with the bullied person. Sometimes girls will rush out of the interviews and be overwhelmingly 'nice' to the bullied pupil. The bullied pupil cannot always cope with this.

Stage 2 Follow-up meetings

The next set of meetings will be to establish how well each pupil has achieved the aim agreed in the first meeting. These are individual meetings, like the first. Although the pupils do not always do exactly what they say they will, they usually will have left the bullied pupil alone. If the bullying has not stopped altogether, you continue to work with the pupils individually to agree a solution to the situation. If it has stopped, congratulate each pupil on their efforts and asks them to continue in the same way. Tell each pupil that the next stage will be a group meeting, and set a date for this.

Stage 3 Group meeting

When stage two is particularly successful, it can be tempting to miss out this third stage. It is, however, this final meeting which leads to an agreement about the long-term maintenance of the change in bullying behaviour. Meet with the bullying pupils briefly first. Ask them to think of some positive statements about the bullied pupil, which can be repeated to the bullied pupil when she or he enters the group. You then fetch the bullied pupil; the seating should be arranged so that the bullied pupil can walk directly to her or his chair without having to walk through the midst of the group. It is usually best if the bullied pupil is sitting next to you.

Remind the pupils how successful they have been in improving the situation. Ask them to suggest ways in which this change can be maintained over time.

You can also encourage the pupils to identify what they will do if someone starts bullying again. By doing this you help them to formulate a 'back-up plan'. Introduce the idea of tolerance, and of living together without quarrelling even if not necessarily being friends. In this way, a long-term agreement is made. You may or may not wish to suggest a further meeting, perhaps in six weeks or the following term, to review the situation. Even if you decide not to meet with the pupils as a group again, follow up the situation after a few weeks to make sure the intervention has been successful.

Strategies for persistent bullying

If used correctly, the Method of Shared Concern usually results in an immediate improvement in the bullying situation. Sometimes, however, there may be one or two members of the bullying gang who consistently use bullying techniques in their peer relationships. They may stop bullying in the short term, but over time they may begin to resume their bullying either of the original pupil or someone else. Additional action is needed for these pupils. Possible strategies might include:

- parental involvement;
- change of class to split the bullying gang;
- personalised behaviour modification plan;
- intensive, individual counselling.

The No Blame Approach: an alternative method

The No Blame Approach was designed by Barbara Maines and George Robinson. The No Blame Approach is similar to the Pikas method in that it emphasises a constructive solution achieved through a participative, non-punitive approach which involves the pupils themselves in resolving the problem. Maines and Robinson, however, focus more on the feelings and status of the pupils involved. Their method has seven steps.

Step 1 Interview the bullied pupil

Talk with the pupil about his or her feelings. Do not question the child directly about the incident, but do try to establish who is involved.

Step 2 Arrange a meeting for all the pupils who are involved

Set up a meeting for all of the pupils who are directly or indirectly involved. Include pupils who joined in but did not directly bully the other child.

Step 3 Explain the problem

Tell the pupils how the bullied child is feeling. You may want to use a drawing or poem or piece of writing written by the pupil to illustrate this. Do not discuss the details of the incident or allocate blame to any of the bullying pupils.

Step 4 Share responsibility

State clearly that you know the group are responsible and can do something about it. Focus on resolving the problem rather than blaming the pupils.

Step 5 Identify solutions

In turn, ask each pupil to suggest a way in which they could help the bullied pupil feel happier in school, show approval of the suggestions but do not ask the pupils to promise to implement their suggestions or go into detail about how they will implement them.

Step 6 Let the pupils take action themselves

End the meeting by giving responsibility to the group to solve the problem. Arrange a time and place to meet again and find how successful they have been.

Step 7 Meet them again

After about a week, see each student and ask how things have been going. It is usually better to see them on their own in order to avoid any new group accusations about who helped and who didn't. The important thing is to ascertain that the bullying has stopped and the bullied pupil is feeling better.

Training

As with the Pikas method, we recommend that you arrange to practice this method with your colleagues before implementing it. Barbara Maines and George Robinson have produced a short training video and Inset booklet for staff to use. This is available from: Lame Duck Publishing Ltd., 10 South Terrace, Redlands, Bristol BS6 6TG.

Assertiveness training for groups of bullied pupils

These groups aim to provide a safe, supportive environment for bullied pupils to talk about their experiences and to learn and practise effective responsive behaviour. Although in this section we will describe the use of assertiveness techniques as used in small group settings, they can also be used with individual pupils or introduced to whole classes within the school.

What is assertive behaviour?

Assertiveness is a set of techniques based on a specific philosophy of human rights. These techniques build on a standard formula and provide an individual with a clearly defined structure to use in professional or social contexts. They therefore provide the user with a 'script' which they can fit to meet their personal needs. We have found that for pupils this script provides a certain sense of security, almost a shield against the nastiness of a bullying situation. Pupils feel more control and power, less anger or despair. They seem able to maintain a neutrality which de-escalates the situation rather than provoking it.

In responding *assertively*, the pupil will stand up for her/his rights without violating the rights of the other pupil. The assertive pupil will respond to the bullying pupil by stating their intentions, wishes and/or feelings clearly and directly. They remain resistant to manipulative or aggressive tactics. Assertive responses not only rely on verbal messages but on eye contact and body language as well.

Setting up an assertiveness group

The training course we have devised, with the help of educational psychologists Tiny Arora and Enid MacNeill, draws on assertive strategies and aims to provide opportunities for pupils to learn and practise these in a safe, supportive environment.

Age

The assertiveness training groups can be held at both primary and secondary level. In the secondary sector, group size can range between four and fifteen. The groups can last from 45 minutes to an hour and a half.

In primary schools, we have worked with pupils aged 7 upwards. It has been our experience that with the younger age groups, it is better to limit the group size to between four and six pupils and the duration of the group to half an hour. It can be helpful to supplement the groupwork with more intensive individual work for some pupils.

Timing

Pupils may be willing to attend in their own time. Running the groups at lunchtime can avoid negative labelling sometimes applied to withdrawal classes. The group assumes the prestige of a club or special activity. It also enables pupils to be more honest about whether they wish to attend or not. Drawbacks are that this limits the time the group can run since the pupils need time to eat lunch therefore often leaving only 30 or 40 minutes. It also depends on teaching staff being willing to give up time. It can also invite curiosity and interruptions from other pupils.

Group composition

Care needs to be taken when deciding on the composition of the group to ensure that the pupils have similar enough experiences to be able to empathise with one another. Where there is great disparity between the bullying experiences of the pupils in the group, e.g. the duration of bullying, the severity of their experiences, etc. it is difficult to move beyond superficial exploration of the bullying situations and this can lead to individual pupils feeling frustrated. Group membership should remain closed after the first session, even if a pupil is recommended to the group by another teacher. If the group runs on a limited cycle of half a term or term, new group members can join at the beginning of the next course.

Identifying bullied pupils

This can be achieved via nominations (by staff, families or pupils themselves) or by surveys. Nominations by staff run the risk of being quite subjective – children who aren't noticed as being 'victims' may be missed out. This can be a particular problem for girls, whose passivity may be seen as 'normal'. Surveys in which pupils identify themselves are equally problematic because, without an assurance of anonymity, pupils do not always admit to being bullied.

Whatever approach is used, you will need to take care that all pupils who may benefit from the group have access to it, and check carefully for any signs of bias in your selection procedure by race, age or gender.

Staffing

Whatever the age of the pupils, we recommend that two adults are involved in the groups. You need not both be teachers but one of you should be experienced as a group facilitator and have knowledge of bullying and assertiveness techniques. With two adults, it is possible to focus closely on individual pupils as well as to assist with modelling the techniques. If one of you is absent for one session, the group can still meet. This continuity can be important for the pupils who may became noticeably possessive about the group.

Duration and content

This kind of support group can run for between six and eight weekly sessions, during which you will teach the pupils how to:

- make assertive statements
- resist manipulation and threats
- respond to name-calling
- leave a bullying situation
- enlist support from bystanders
- boost their own self-esteem
- remain calm in stressful situations.

Aim to allow opportunities for pupils to explore alternative strategies appropriate to the particular bullying situations they currently face or previous situations which they would have preferred to have handled differently.

Teaching methods

The method for teaching them these techniques is based on maximising the opportunities for modelling and practice within the group setting. The pupils need to feel familiar with the 'script' they are being taught to enhance their confidence in using it. Introduce one assertive technique per session. A successful process for introducing each technique is described in **Information Box 5.4**.

There may sometimes be a need to work individually with some members of the group to assist them in fully establishing the technique. You can also broaden the discussion to consider how to predict when bullying might occur and how to avoid it. Some pupils may be experiencing difficulties with their peers because they use inappropriate social skills. With these pupils you may wish to add some additional activities to teach them how to make friends or how to join in.

One of the concerns often raised about this kind of groupwork, is to what extent the pupils generalise their learning beyond the boundaries of the group. To assist the process of generalisation, allow repetition of each technique applied to different situations. Each pupil has the opportunity to rehearse using the technique to resolve or resist their own personal bullying situations.

The importance of rehearsal

One common feature of bullying behaviour is that it is persistent (Smith and Thompson, 1991). The bullying situations faced by these pupils may have been continuing for some time. Within the group, each pupil can prepare themselves gradually for applying the appropriate technique outside the group. They themselves

INFORMATION BOX 5.4   INTRODUCING AND PRACTISING A TECHNIQUE

- Sitting in a circle, ask each pupil in turn to try out a bullying demand on you. Respond to each individual using the assertive script being introduced. Each pupil will hear the script being used several times before they themselves actually use it.
- Ask each pupil in turn to repeat the script with the next person round the circle. This enables you to observe each pupil practising the technique and give feedback on accuracy, tone, eye contact, etc. The pupils continue to familiarise themselves with the technique.
- In pairs or threes, ask the pupils to experiment with the technique, using situations from their own lives. The third pupil can observe and provide feedback on facial expression, body posture, etc.
- As a whole group invite the pupils to share difficult situations from their personal experiences where the technique might have been helpful. Role-play some of these situations; discuss how effective the technique was.
- Finish with whole-group discussion about applications of the technique. In this stage, fears or anxieties of the pupils about 'when it might not work' can be examined and strategies suggested.

choose the moment to put a particular strategy into practice and this can be discussed and evaluated within the group context. You may find that in some secondary-aged groups, the pupils form informal support networks which extend beyond the group meetings. You may wish to encourage these friendships.

A combination of rehearsal based on real life experiences and discussion of when and how the pupils will put the techniques into practice may assist with the generalisation process. Include opportunities for rehearsal in non-school-based situations, e.g. around the neighbourhood or at the shops as well as school-based situations.

The first and last session

Opening and closing the group is important. In the first session pupils are likely to feel unconfident and nervous; in the last they may be reluctant to end and feel a sense of loss.

In the first session, introductions should be made and the ground rules for the group established. Confidentiality is an important issue. Pupils are free to describe group *activities* to anyone outside the group, and to share their *own* personal information, but they should not pass on *other* people's personal information.

ACTIVITY BOX 5.1   GETTING TO KNOW EACH OTHER

Best foot forward

Each pupil receives two A3 pieces of paper and some coloured pens. They are asked to draw around their feet (with or without shoes). They choose one foot to be their 'best foot' and one to be their 'not so good foot'. On the best foot, they draw or write all the things they like about themselves; things that they enjoy doing or that make them feel happy; things they are good at. On the not so good foot they draw or write things they don't like or make them worried, angry or upset; things they find difficult. Advise the pupils not to put down anything they don't want other people to know about because they will be telling the rest of the group about their feet. It is a good idea if before the pupils begin to work on their feet, you show them yours prepared earlier. Allow the pupils 10 to 15 minutes to work on their feet. Some pupils may need some prompts for ideas. When everyone has finished their feet, they return to the circle. Each person introduces themselves via their feet.

The pupils will be working closely together for the next 6 to 8 weeks and may be talking about very personal experiences. This first meeting should offer opportunities for them to talk about themselves and get to know each other. A safe and fun activity for doing this is called 'Best foot forward . . .' (see **Activity Box 5.1**).

Sometimes, pupils describe their not so good foot last. To make sure that the session ends on a good note finish off with 'boasting', an activity to boost self-esteem.

ACTIVITY BOX 5.2   BOASTING

Ask each member of the group to think of three things they like about themselves. With a partner, they have to look the person in the eyes and say confidently and clearly, 'I am [name] and I am good at . . .'. You should go first. Once they have practised with their neighbour, ask each pupil to boast to the rest of the group.

Closing the group needs to be handled sensitively and perhaps marked by a specific activity or event. 'I will . . . I can . . .' statements or 'Traffic Lights' make positive closing activities (see **Activity Box 5.3**).

ACTIVITY BOX 5.3   CLOSING ACTIVITIES

'I will . . . I can' statements

Each pupil reflects back over the previous sessions and decides on two positive changes they will try to make once the group is over. Each pupil in the group takes it in turn to say what they will and what they can do from now on.

Traffic lights

Each pupil receives three circles of paper – one red, one amber, one green. On the green circle they write or draw something that they have learnt from the group that they will start doing immediately; on the amber circle they write or draw something they have learnt from the group that they think will be useful sometimes; on the red circle they write or draw something that they have learnt from the group that will be a major and long-lasting personal change.

The techniques

These techniques have been selected from the range of assertiveness work to help bullied pupils in particular. It is important for children to rehearse them and apply them to their own situations. They will have to learn to judge whether or not a particular technique is right for their situation.

Always encourage the pupils to be assertive but remind them that they should not be afraid to seek support from their peers or from an adult. Also teach them that they should take the earliest opportunity to leave the situation.

Advise the pupils to:

- be assertive;
- enlist support;
- leave the situation as quickly as possible.

After they have left the situation, they should tell a teacher or parent what has happened.

Be assertive!

Body language and eye contact

All of the assertiveness techniques described in the next section depend on a combination of verbal message *and* confident body language. When responding assertively to a situation, pupils should stand upright and look the other person in the eye. The pupil's facial expression should be neutral, smiling only if appropriate. Hands and arms should be relaxed and by the side or in pockets. Crossed arms, covering the mouth with a hand or fidgeting are defensive behaviours. Hands on hips or pointing can be perceived as aggressive. Many bullied pupils need to practise how to talk to people as well as what to say.

Assertive statements

Making an assertive statement involves being clear, honest and direct. It involves stating quite specifically and calmly what you want or how you feel about an event or situation. For example, a pupil might be being disturbed by another pupil who is talking noisily while she/he wants to work. An assertive response would be, 'I would like you to be quiet'; an aggressive response would be 'Shut up or I'll hit you'; a passive response would be to suffer in silence or to move. For bullied pupils, assertive statements can be helpful when responding to name-calling, teasing or mild physical provocation. Pupils can learn to say, 'I don't like it when you do that. I want you to stop.'

Resisting manipulation and threats

When children are under pressure they can choose between two assertive techniques. The first is to say 'No' or even 'No, I don't want to'; the second is slightly more sophisticated and is based upon the repetition of an assertive statement.

Learning to say 'No' can be harder than it sounds. Children, especially girls, are often encouraged to be 'kind' and 'unselfish'. Unfortunately, this can sometimes lead to children doing things against their wishes or best interests. To be able to say 'No', children have to learn that they have the right to say 'No' and also when to use that right. If they feel comfortable complying with another person's request, then they should say 'Yes'. They also may be able to identify a compromise solution that will keep everybody happy. If, however, they have that sinking feeling of 'Oh, no, I really don't want to do this', then they should say 'No'.

Manipulation, threat and persuasion are often based on moral or emotional reasoning. Common statements used to pressure children into doing things they don't want to include:

- I'll tell on you.
- I won't be your friend any more.
- I'll tell the rest of the class a secret about you.
- I'll get my brother/sister on you.
- I'll get you after school.
- Go on, it's only this once.
- That's not fair, I lent you mine.
- Chicken! What a wimp!

It can be hard for a child to stand up to a barrage of such threats and promises. One way of resisting is to keep repeating the same assertive statement until the other children give up asking. This technique is called 'broken record' because it is reminiscent of a record being stuck. Here is an example of 'broken record' in practice.

Rachel Lend us your bike, Lou.
Lou I don't lend my bike.
Rachel Go on, don't be such a spoil sport!
Lou I don't lend my bike.
Rachel But I lent you mine the other day.
Lou I don't lend my bike.
Rachel I won't let you go on my computer!
Lou I like your computer but I don't lend my bike.
Rachel I give up!

The broken record here was 'I don't lend my bike'. Prepare the pupils for the physical intimidation which might accompany this kind of threat or manipulation. Teach the pupils to remain confident even if the bullying pupil does come very close or give nasty looks. Usually, the other pupil will stop pressuring the child using broken record after three attempts. Nevertheless, children who are being taught this kind of technique against bullying also need to assess when is the best time to walk away from the situation. Practise the technique, *and* walking away!

Responding to name-calling

If assertively telling the other person to stop name-calling does not work, then a technique called 'fogging' can be helpful. When fogging, the bullied pupil responds to each taunt or name with a neutral statement which aims to de-escalate the situation rather than escalate it. Statements such as 'You might think so'; 'Possibly'; 'It might look that way to you'; 'So?' are fogging-type statements. The tormentor soon becomes fatigued if the bullied pupil remains calm and nonchalant in the face of their abuse.

Sometimes pupils are faced with situations where more than one or two people are calling names and it not appropriate to stop and 'fog'. Perhaps, they are walking along the school corridor or out of the toilets and a large crowd of pupils are sniggering and making comments. In these situations, children can be taught to 'positive self talk' – just as it sounds, this involves saying nice things to yourself! By concentrating mentally on positive messages such as 'I can stay calm', 'I am wonderful', etc., it is possible to block out external messages to a certain extent. Within the assertiveness group, pupils can practise this by walking through the rest of the group whilst you walk alongside them actually saying positive statements in her/his ear which were chosen earlier by the pupil herself or himself. The pupil can then try it out unaided.

When working on name-calling activities with pupils, it is worthwhile devising a 'nasty name bank'. This consists of an envelope or bag with individual slips of paper, upon each slip is a nasty name. You can create the bank yourself or make it with the pupils. Having a nasty name bank depersonalises the names used – everybody knows that it is an exercise to learn how to cope with name-calling and the names being used do not reflect upon them personally.

Enlist support!

Emphasise that if the pupils are being bullied, they do not *have* to resolve the situation by themselves. Whilst you do not want them to rely totally on others all the time as this can be disempowering, they can be helped by their peers and by staff to stand up to the bullying pupils. There may be other pupils or adults who are nearby during a bullying incident. Shouting to attract their attention can quickly put an end to the incident and provide back up for assertive behaviour. Statements such as 'Look what they're doing! It's not fair, is it?' can mobilise bystanders into activity and create an instant challenge to the bullying behaviour.

Although pretending a passer-by is a relative or running into a shop are not assertive behaviours, such 'tricks' can provide temporary relief from a bullying situation. Check that all the pupils in your group know basic safety codes, such as how to call the police (and that these calls are free).

In the long term, pupils who are being persistently bullied by their peers can ask individuals to support them if it happens again. Approaching peers who, whilst not involved directly, can often be bystanders, can lead to increased bystander support in the future. Within the group, pupils can identify who might be supportive and rehearse how they will approach them.

Leave the situation as quickly as possible!

This is best done quickly and calmly. Through role-play, pupils can reconstruct the bullying situations they have encountered. Within the group, they can then re-play them but this time introducing the appropriate assertiveness techniques. They also need to practise when and how to walk away. Actually looking at walking styles and body language can be helpful. Teach the pupils to walk confidently and unhesitatingly, having looked their tormentor in the eye. If possible, choose an exit to the side rather than backing off or pushing past the bullying pupils. There may be times when the most prudent action is to run away as fast as possible. Discuss with the pupils how they should choose which course of action to take.

There will be times when pupils may be crowded by the bullying pupils and there is no clear exit. Enlisting the support of bystanders can help if there are other people around. Alternatively, pupils can be taught how to use a combination of body weight and strategy to push through the group without being violent. By crossing their hands in front of their bodies in line with the chest bone, pupils can push forwards and down between two of the crowding pupils, applying pressure at the point where the crowd is weak and therefore creating a gap. The other pupils may react very quickly and try to close the gap but are likely to create another gap elsewhere by doing this. Once clear of the crowd, the pupil should leave as quickly as possible and tell an adult at the earliest opportunity.

Local community police officers or women's self-defence groups may be able to assist you in running a session on safe techniques for resisting physical violence. Unfortunately, bullied pupils do sometimes find themselves in life-threatening or otherwise potentially harmful situations. They need to be equipped to handle this.

Boosting their own self-esteem

Throughout the assertiveness group, it is worthwhile working on building self-esteem. Activities which involve giving and receiving compliments; positive self-statements; circle activities where each pupil completes a sentence such as 'I like myself because I . . .' etc. help to remind the pupils that they are valued human beings.

Remaining calm in stressful situations

Teaching children how to relax helps them to stay calm, and therefore appear confident, in bullying situations. There are many strategies available for stress management and relaxation. They usually fall into three categories:

- breathing control;
- physical relaxation;
- visualisation.

ACTIVITY BOX 5.4   RELAXATION TECHNIQUES

Breathing control

Ask the pupils to take a slow, deep breath in. They should try to fill their lungs right to the bottom so they are really full of air. When they are full, ask them to hold their breath for the count of three and slowly exhale. They should try to breathe out more slowly than they breathed in. Repeat three times. Remind them not to worry about being noisy. They should be encouraged to breathe through their noses if possible; if not, they should breathe through slightly parted lips.

Physical relaxation

Physical relaxation can be achieved by tensing a muscle, holding it tense for a few seconds and then releasing the tension. Initially, you might practise with a hand. Each pupil clenches their hand tightly into a fist; holds it tense for the count of three and then lets it flop. Once they are used to the idea, you can begin to work on the whole body. The pupils should be sitting or standing – they are unlikely to be lying down in school! Work through each muscle group, tensing it; holding the tension; relaxing it. Start with the feet and legs; then work up to the stomach and buttocks; then hands and arms; take three deep breaths to relax the rib cage and chest; shrug the shoulders three times to relax shoulders and upper back; shrug them forwards across the chest to relax the shoulder blades; swallow to relax the neck; finally tense the face muscles; hold and relax. Having worked each muscle group individually, pupils can tense and relax the whole body at once. Try to encourage them to recognise extra tense points: jaw, stomach, neck and shoulders are often particularly vulnerable to stress.

Visualisation

Mental images can help with keeping calm. Once physically relaxed, pupils can be asked to build up a mental picture of somewhere they feel safe, secure and confident in themselves. They need to work hard at picturing the colours, sounds, smells, sensations, feelings which accompany the place. When tense, they can revisualise the place and re-experience the feelings of security and confidence.

For pupils who find visualisation difficult, mentally counting slowly to ten and back again can help people to regain control and reduce stress.

Maintaining assertive behaviour

A 6- or 8-week course can be effective in providing pupils with helpful strategies against bullying. Badly bullied pupils, who have low self-esteem and poor self-confidence, may need additional 'booster' sessions over time. By maintaining intermittent contact with the pupils, you will be able monitor how effectively they are coping with difficult situations in school. Some pupils may need more intensive individual work to consolidate the skills learnt within the group.

Assertiveness training is most fully effective when used in conjunction with other strategies. Work with all pupils to encourage rejection of bullying values within the peer group and work with the bullying pupils to stop and prevent further bullying incidents need to run alongside the assertiveness training for bullied pupils.

SUMMARY

In this chapter we have considered ways of intervening in bullying situations and for supporting bullied pupils. Schools we have worked with have found these strategies effective but remember that no one strategy is *always* successful. You will need to develop a range of strategies for responding to bullying. Bullying is a complex social problem and as such requires a multi-faceted approach to combat it. You, your staff and your pupils should be clear about what will happen next if the bullying persists.

S·I·X | how to prevent and respond to bullying behaviour in the junior/ middle school playground

MICHAEL BOULTON

Bullying is likely to be a feature of most if not all junior/middle schools and the playground is likely to be the most common location in which such anti-social behaviour will be carried out. It is still not entirely clear why so much of the bullying that occurs in school should take place on the playground, but several factors seem likely. Playgrounds tend to be lightly supervised, and often the ratio of children to playground supervisors exceeds 50:1. Increased supervision and patrol by adults may help, but I shall argue that we will probably deceive ourselves if we believe that such a simple step will go far enough. Bullying is such a complicated category of behaviour, with complex and varied causes, that mere 'policing' may not be the best response we can make to it. As an example, we now know that acts of bullying on the playground go beyond the stereotypical forms of physical assaults that many adults expect bullying to take. **Information Box 6.1** illustrates some of the many ways that children on the junior/middle school playground have been observed to bully their fellow pupils. The upshot of this – that bullying can take a range of different forms, some that don't even involve any physical contact – is that even if there were more adults on the playground at break times, many instances of bullying would still be likely to go unnoticed.

All pupils can be harmed by these sort of experience. There may also be long-term effects of bullying (see Chapter 1).

Tackling playground bullying should be high on the agenda for junior/middle

---

INFORMATION BOX 6.1   EXAMPLES OF PLAYGROUND BULLYING

- An 11-year-old boy presses an 11-year-old male victim up against a wall and punches the victim repeatedly and with much force in the chest. The victim struggles to escape and does so after 2 minutes.
- A 10-year-old boy prods an 11-year-old female victim lightly but repeatedly in the chest with a forefinger, until she begins to cry.
- A group of 8-year-old girls repeatedly exclude a female victim of the same age from their games of skipping.
- A group of 11-year-old girls spread the rumour that a female victim of the same age wets herself.
- A group of 10-year-old boys repeatedly take money and sweets from a pair of 8-year-old male victims, and say, 'This is OK isn't it? You don't mind do you?' The younger boys are too frightened to tell anybody about this.
- A group of 9-year-old girls persistently tease an 11-year-old boy by calling him a wimp.

---

schools, but the task of doing so will be far from easy. We may never totally eliminate bullying and other anti-social behaviour. Indeed, the Elton Report stated that 'Reducing bad behaviour is a realistic aim; eliminating it completely is not' (DES, 1989, 2:28). Rather than be disheartened by this point of view, I believe that we should draw inspiration from it. Whatever the level of bullying is in a given school, there is likely to be *something* that can be done to reduce it by some amount. My aim in this section is to show that steps, some of them simple and easy to execute, others more complex and demanding, can be taken to reduce playground bullying, and to give some practical advice as to how begin.

Understanding bullying in the playground

The presence/absence of bullying in the playground is influenced by a myriad of individual but often related factors. The children themselves, the playground supervisors and the physical nature of the playground interact in extremely complex, and as yet not clearly understood, ways. **Figure 6.1** captures just some of the complexities involved in trying to determine causal pathways in playground bullying, and hence some of the reasons why flexibility in selecting interventions is necessary.

Although many schools will share the common problem of playground bullying,

INFORMATION BOX 6.2 CHILDREN'S COMMENTS ABOUT BEING BULLIED ON THE PLAYGROUND

- 'I hate playtime. Gary's gang always pick on me and call me horrible names and spoil my games. I wish I could stay in at break.' (11-year-old girl)
- 'I don't like this school 'cos the big kids hit me. They do it all the time in the playground. If I was big I'd bash 'em'. (8-year-old boy)
- 'The worst thing about this school is what goes on in the yard. You wouldn't believe it but so many kids are picking on the other kids. They pick on me sometimes just because I use an inhaler. They call me 'Inhaler, inhaler, inhaler'. It drives me mad'. (10-year-old boy)
- 'Just because I'm Asian some of the White kids pick on me. I know they are stupid, and I try to ignore them but it wears you down. Every day is the same. I go home for dinner now so I miss most of it. But it means I can't play with Gulshan and my other friends'. (11-year-old girl)

they are likely to be unique in terms of the specific factors that could be responsible for bullying behaviour, and/or in terms of the action that they can take. For example, your school may be 'lucky' enough to have sufficient playground space for children to be able to spread themselves out, on the other hand your school might be very restricted in this respect. Teachers in schools with large playgrounds often complain that these are very barren places that are exposed to the elements, and that this harsh environment makes bullying more likely. Teachers in schools where playground space is limited often report that children have to 'compete' with one another for space, and this can lead to fights and arguments which in turn precipitate bullying.

Your school may already have tried to do something about playground bullying, or you may only just be becoming aware that it is a major problem.

This section presents a 'menu' of things that schools could do. You can therefore select *for yourselves* which interventions you would like to implement. Some of these interventions require supervisors or teachers to be involved in short meetings or training events. Arrangements for payment of lunchtime supervisors' cover will need to be made but the financial costs are small when you consider the potential benefits.

The rest of this chapter will outline a variety of practical steps that you can take to reduce the amount of playground bullying. Some of these suggestions have come from talking with teachers and lunchtime supervisors, some from our own experiences on the DFE Sheffield Anti-Bullying Project, and some from other workers in this field.

The suggestions are presented under a number of broad headings, but you should view these as guidelines only – there is no reason why you should not select ideas from the different sections to build your own intervention programme.

Raising the status of lunchtime supervisors with pupils

It has been said that playtime is the forgotten part of the school day. Similarly, lunchtime supervisors are sometimes the forgotten element in the personnel of schools. There are probably many and varied reasons for this, but it would seem that even today lunchtime supervisors are not always perceived as having the same authority as teachers by families. In the words of one lunchtime supervisor:

> It's terrible out there on the playground. The children have no respect for us at all. Just the other day, a little 8-year-old boy swore at me. They wouldn't dare use language like that in front of their teachers.

There can be little doubt that whatever causes many children to view lunch time supervisors in such a negative way, the fact that they do will affect what happens on the playground. For example, it will influence what type of behaviour pupils will show in front of the lunchtime supervisors, as well as how they will respond to the directions of the supervisors. Anyone perceived as having little authority will not act as a deterrent for children predisposed to bullying or other anti-social behaviour. Furthermore, directions from such individuals are more likely to be ignored compared to those that come from clear figures of authority, such as teachers.

Raising the status of lunchtime supervisors with children will help them to come to appreciate that *all* people are important, and help to dispel the perception, which some schools may unwittingly perpetuate, that some individuals or groups matter less than others and hence can be the targets for inconsiderate behaviour.

In many schools, then, there is a clear need to improve the perceptions of lunchtime supervisors by pupils. How this might be achieved is shown in **Activity Box 6.1**.

You could also ensure that the rewards supervisors can give to children are the same as those used by members of the teaching staff. For example, if a school or a class has a system whereby exceptionally good behaviour is rewarded by points, then supervisors should be in a position to give points in this way. The fact that such a continuity is not a feature of most schools may be one, albeit small, reason why so much misbehaviour occurs in the playground – it may give the impression that playground behaviour is less important than classroom behaviour.

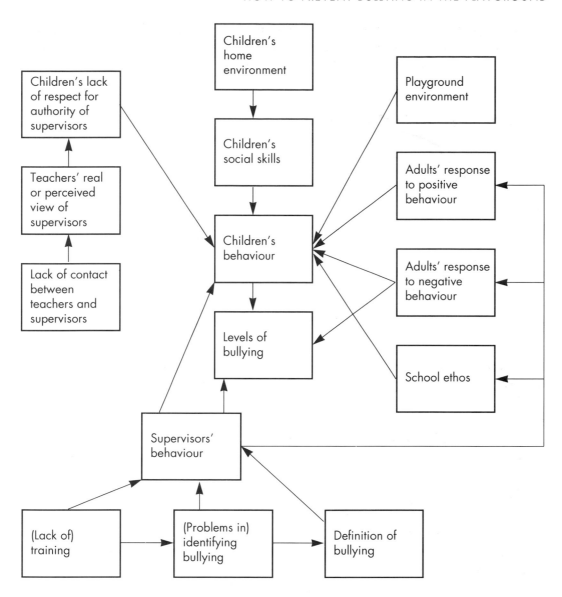

Figure 6.1 Some of the factors thought to be involved in playground bullying

ACTIVITY BOX 6.1 RAISING THE STATUS OF LUNCHTIME SUPERVISORS WITH PUPILS

After first consulting with the lunchtime supervisors and gaining their approval, the headteacher or another senior manager introduces them to pupils. Inform the pupils that supervisors have the same level of authority as members of the teaching staff. Make explicit how pupils are expected to respond to their requests.

This introduction could take place during a formal assembly, preferably at the start of each school year, to reinforce the importance of the lunchtime supervisors.

Give the supervisors name badges to wear when they are in school (again, only after their approval has been obtained). Encourage pupils to address supervisors by their name. In order to reinforce the notion that supervisors have the same level of authority as teachers, adopt the same system used to address teachers.

Building better relationships between supervisors and pupils

Establishing the rightful status of lunchtime supervisors with children, partly by means of introductions, formal ways of addressing them, and by making explicit how they should be responded to, would also be a step towards enhancing relationships between the supervisors and the pupils. There are good reasons for proposing that good relationships between supervisors and pupils will help to reduce levels of bullying:

- Many children are reluctant to tell an adult if they, or any of their peers are being bullied. By enhancing relationships, children may be more likely to tell supervisors when things like bullying take place.
- Supervisors will probably find it easier to assert their authority over disruptive pupils if the pupils are known to them. For example, a child is more likely to respond to the directions of a supervisor if she/he is addressed by name ('If I see you doing that again Michael X, I'll give you a yellow card') rather than in an anonymous manner ('If I see you doing that again, I'll give you a yellow card').
- Good relationships between pupils and lunchtime supervisors may also discourage bullying. A child who values the opinion of a lunchtime supervisor may be less likely to engage in bullying.

One method for promoting good relationships between pupils and lunchtime supervisors is to link a supervisor with a specific class or classes in school (see **Activity Box 6.2**).

ACTIVITY BOX 6.2   PROMOTING GOOD RELATIONSHIPS
BETWEEN PUPILS AND LUNCHTIME SUPERVISORS

Link up lunchtime supervisors and class teachers. Invite the supervisor to
come into the appropriate classroom, at a time agreed with the class teacher,
and work with the pupils. For example, she/he could hear them read, read to
them or help them with their school work.

A more specific way of enhancing relationships between pupils and
lunchtime supervisors is by means of a pupil project. In conjunction with the
class teacher, the lunchtime supervisor helps the pupils, who are working in
small groups, to plan a project to investigate 'a day in the life of a lunchtime
supervisor'. This might involve shadowing and interviews, perhaps of other
supervisors who have been paired with another class.

The familiarity engendered by this sort of contact may promote better
relationships, as well as fostering an appreciation of some of the difficulties
faced by supervisors.

Building better relationships between supervisors and teachers

We have seen that supervisors are not typically viewed in a positive way by many children, and argued that this should be a cause for concern. It also appears that some
teachers and senior staff do not fully recognise the important contribution that
lunchtime supervisors make to the management of children's behaviour. At an
extreme level, one teacher argued that:

> Sometimes they [lunchtime supervisors] make things worse. They don't seem to
> know how to handle the children.

Another comment was that:

> Dinner ladies have it easy on the playground. Most of the time the kids are only
> playing and they [the lunchtime supervisors] stand around chatting.

My own observations on school playgrounds, and interviews with lunchtime supervisors, suggest that in many, if not all cases, these sorts of comments are, at the very
least only partially true, and at worst, doing supervisors a great disservice. The vast
majority of lunchtime supervisors offer a great deal of commitment to their work.
Hence lunchtime supervisors and their dedication to their work remain a largely

---

ACTIVITY BOX 6.3   RAISING TEACHERS' AWARENESS OF THE PROBLEMS FACED BY LUNCHTIME SUPERVISORS

Ask a senior manager or other interested member of the teaching staff to arrange a special staff meeting in which it is explained to the lunchtime supervisors and other members of the school's teaching staff why better links between them would be desirable. Following this briefing, invite the supervisors to a subsequent meeting where they are given the opportunity to give a presentation outlining the major problems that they face in their particular school. Following the presentation, teachers and supervisors could engage in discussions leading to agreement about resolution of the problems.

A member of the teaching staff and a member of the supervisory staff could act as co-ordinators, to prepare and circulate a broad agenda for the second and subsequent meetings, and to discuss facilities such as flip charts and OHP.

For this suggestion to be effective, there must be commitment from teaching staff and senior managers to translate the outcome of the meeting into action.

---

untapped resource in our quest to remove bullying from the junior/middle school playground. There are several ways that negative teacher perceptions of lunchtime supervisors can be remedied, and some of these are described in this chapter.

On a general level, good relationships between lunchtime supervisors and members of the teaching staff would be beneficial in terms of preventing playground bullying for several reasons.

First, it will facilitate information being exchanged about which specific children have engaged in bullying activities and some potential reasons why this occurred. Teaching staff could then follow up incidents reported to them by supervisors. Supervisors could also be informed by teachers of any problems that might influence a child's playground behaviour.

Second, it will facilitate consistency in the way adults respond to unacceptable behaviour. For example, the supervisors and teachers can agree which things should always be reported to the other group and/or to the senior management. Bullying would be on this list along with such things as racist remarks and acts of vandalism.

ACTIVITY BOX 6.4   TEACHER/SUPERVISOR SHADOWING

Each teacher is invited to spend a lunchtime shadowing the supervisor with whom she/he is paired, and the supervisor spends one or more lessons in class with the teacher (possibly combined with the suggestions of **Activity Box 6.2**).

When the teacher is shadowing the supervisor on the playground, it is very important that she/he does not undermine the status of the supervisor in the eyes of the pupils by taking control of situations in which children misbehave. The intention is for the teacher to witness the many and varied everyday problems that the supervisor has to deal with. In this way, each member of the pair should gain a better insight into the problems faced by the other, and of the valuable contribution they each make to the education and well-being of the pupils.

Follow up the shadowing exercise with a subsequent staff meeting where issues raised by both teachers and supervisors can be discussed. In the long term, organise brief meetings between lunchtime supervisors and teachers to discuss any other aspects of the children's behaviour that they feel are causes for concern.

Raising teacher's awareness of the problems faced by lunchtime supervisors

Teachers and senior managers are not always fully aware of the day-to-day problems faced by lunchtime supervisors. After all, teachers and senior managers have their own concerns and are working under different pressures. At the same time lunchtime supervisors are not always fully aware of the pressures teachers are under. **Activity Box 6.3** outlines a suggestion for raising teachers' awareness of the problems faced by lunchtime supervisors.

Teacher/supervisor shadowing exercise

Another way in which good relationships between lunchtime supervisors and teachers can be built up is by means of a shadowing exercise. Some suggestions for how this might be implemented are shown in **Activity Box 6.4**.

> **ACTIVITY BOX 6.5**   'STAFF IS EVERYBODY'
>
> The term 'staff' is clearly understood to include *all* staff within a school.
>   Ensure that if any communication, etc. is directed towards only one section of the school's staff, then this is clearly made explicit, such as 'teaching staff', 'supervisory staff', 'catering staff', etc.

Adopting a 'staff is everybody' philosophy

Another factor that may undermine relationships between lunchtime supervisors and teachers is the implicit view that some sections of the school's staff are more important than others. Try to view your school as a single community in which every section contributes something *essential* to it's day-to-day operation. To this end, you should work towards a 'staff is everybody' approach (see **Activity Box 6.5**).

Increased liaison between teaching staff and supervisors at the end of lunch break

It is common in most junior/middle schools (and secondary schools) for there to be little or no contact between supervisors and members of the teaching staff at the end of the lunch break. Typically, a teacher (or teachers) enters the playground at the very end of the break, blows a whistle (or gives a similar signal) to indicate that playtime is over, and the supervisors leave the playground to have their lunch. This does not allow time for information to be passed either about how any given child has behaved in the playground or relevant personal information about the child's well-being.

   By creating opportunities for increased contact, you will facilitate better handling of individual pupils and avoid inconsistency which may lead to more serious problems.

Training courses for lunchtime supervisors

In most schools in the UK, teachers are only employed after they have undergone extensive periods of training, and this is usually supplemented by regular in-service courses. The situation is very different for most lunchtime supervisors. They are not required to have undergone any formal training and many do not attend the relatively few training courses that are available. This situation is wholly unacceptable for many reasons, not least because lunchtime supervisors are faced with, and have to manage, some of the most difficult types of behaviour that children engage in when they are in school. Bullying would be high on this list of problem behaviour. Many supervisors, though by no means all, have children of their own, and are likely to employ strategies in their professional life that they use with their own children. Unfortunately, what works in the relatively narrow confines of family life may not be so successful in the playground. Indeed, some tactics may actually exacerbate children's problem behaviours. Clearly there is need for lunchtime supervisors to be offered the opportunity to attend training courses designed to enhance their child management skills.

In response to this need, Sonia Sharp and I set out to design a basic training course for lunchtime supervisors that was specifically related to the issue of playground bullying. This course consisted of two sessions each of about two and a half hours duration. Some of the issues that we thought should be raised in such a training programme, and some of the activities the supervisors were encouraged to participate in, are outlined in the rest of this section. You may wish to develop a similar course for your own supervisors. It can be helpful for supervisors to meet with supervisors from other schools. You may consider linking with other local schools to offer a joint training day.

Introducing the lunchtime supervisors to the training programme

In the first session, the lunchtime supervisors were introduced to the course leaders, who gave a brief presentation on the theme 'Why we are here'. This presentation reiterated to the supervisors that the senior management within their particular school recognised the importance of their role, and in a non-patronising way pointed out that all lunchtime supervisors have a valuable contribution to make to the reduction of problem behaviours that occur on the school playground. These and related points were used to make the case that, like other members of the school personnel, lunchtime supervisors deserve to have the opportunity to attend training courses.

Encouraging lunchtime supervisors to recognise their valuable contribution to managing children's behaviour

Our first training session also involved a group activity designed to reinforce the view that lunchtime supervisors are essential for the smooth running of schools and the well-being of pupils (**Activity Box 6.6**). We believe that this is an important exercise given the low status of lunchtime supervisors in many schools.

Another group activity involves the lunchtime supervisors identifying behavioural problems in the playground (**Activity Box 6.7**). Again, this exercise is useful because

---

ACTIVITY BOX 6.6   THE VALUE OF LUNCHTIME SUPERVISORS

Ask the supervisors to form small groups, ideally with supervisors from the same school separating from one another and joining those from other schools.

The groups are then asked to consider, and make brief notes on, two issues:

• What they thought would happen if a school did not have lunchtime supervisors;
• Why they as lunchtime supervisors make a valuable contribution to their particular school.

The points raised during the small group discussions are then presented to the group as a whole for further comment.

ACTIVITY BOX 6.7   PROBLEM BEHAVIOURS IN THE PLAYGROUND

Supervisors are asked to form small groups, and then to make a list of the many separate problems that they encounter in their role as playground supervisors.

They are also asked to indicate which they thought were the most serious problems, and which they thought were less serious.

The small groups report back to the group as a whole, and give their reasons for viewing some problems as more or less serious than others.

---

it highlights that some problems, such as bullying, are likely to be common to most/all schools regardless of their specific characteristics, whereas other problems may be unique to particular schools. It also shows that while many issues associated with the way children behave on the playground are important, some may require more urgent attention than others.

Basic knowledge about bullying

All of the small groups of lunchtime supervisors that took part in the activity designed to highlight playground behaviour problems had bullying on their list of serious transgressions. This offered a useful and logical lead in to another part of our first training session, namely a brief presentation on facts and figures about bullying by

---

ACTIVITY BOX 6.8   WHAT IS MEANT BY BULLYING

Bullying has been defined in different ways by different people. Ask the supervisors to work in small groups. Invite each group to discuss what they understand by the term 'bullying'. They may use their own personal experiences of bullying, either as adults or children to help them to identify what bullying is.

   After about 10 to 15 minutes, ask members of each group to agree on a definition. Ask the supervisors to present their definition for discussion to the group as a whole.

---

members of the project team. Some of the important points that we covered included facts and figures about bullying on the playground, some consequences of bullying for young children, and some common myths about bullying. The information presented can be found in Chapter 2 of this handbook.

Defining what is meant by bullying

Some of the other small group activities that we used in our training sessions with lunchtime supervisors focused on highlighting some of the problems associated with defining bullying. One approach was simply to invite small groups of supervisors to informally discuss what they meant by the term 'bullying' (see **Activity Box 6.8**). Another activity used successfully with supervisors was the 'Defining Bullying' Activity described in Chapter 3 'Establishing a whole-school anti-bullying policy'.

   The ultimate aim of definition-seeking activities, such as those described in **Activity Box 6.8**, is to foster consensus about what actual behaviours should be viewed as bullying, and hence those that will not be tolerated on the playground. One common outcome of such exercises is that stereotyped definitions of bullying can be challenged. Often people have an image of the typical bully as a physically robust boy who physically assaults smaller and/or weaker pupils. As we have seen, bullying and pupils who bully may come in many different forms, and other less obvious types of bullying may be just as upsetting, or even lead to greater levels of distress than hitting and kicking.

   Encourage lunchtime supervisors to agree among themselves on this issue, or at least discuss it, and then contribute their views to the whole-school policy on bullying, which also covers this theme (see Chapter 3).

Problems in trying to correctly identify bullying on the playground

Our first training session with the lunchtime supervisors also involved a presentation and discussion on practical problems associated with trying to identify bullying when it occurs on the playground. Basically, there are two types of error that can be made – false negative errors and false positive errors.

- A false negative error occurs when it is decided that a child was not bullying another child when she/he actually was.
- A false positive error occurs when it is decided that a child was bullying another child when she/he actually was not doing so.

INFORMATION BOX 6.3   PROBLEMS IN IDENTIFYING BULLYING – AN EXAMPLE OF A SITUATION IN WHICH A SUPERVISOR DID NOT SEE THE WHOLE SITUATION

Case study

Jamie (aged 11 years) was playing with his friends of the same age when Daniel (also 11 years old) approached him and began to bully him. The bullying took a variety of different forms including teasing, light taps and powerful punches to the chest and arms. Jamie's friends tried to stop Daniel but were driven away by him. After about 15 minutes, Jamie began to fight back for the first time and he wrestled Daniel to the ground. Just at that moment, a lunchtime supervisor walked past the boys and immediately went up to them and disciplined Jamie. Jamie was taken into school to see the headteacher, despite his protestations of innocence. Daniel was not punished and he went over to his friends and explained what had happened. They all agreed that this incident was highly amusing.

Analysis and suggestions

Situations in which the supervisor has not seen the whole of an incident are especially problematic to deal with, simply because the 'facts' about what actually went on are incomplete. Unfortunately, this type of situation is likely to occur fairly frequently, given that lunchtime supervisors are often in charge of a large number of pupils. It would be tempting to assume that what was actually observed gives an accurate representation of the whole situation, but supervisors would be advised to resist such a temptation. The aim should be to gather information about what actually happened *prior* to coming to a decision and taking action. Some or all of the following tactics have worked for other supervisors and you might like to try them yourselves.

Supervisor Jamie, what is happening here? Daniel looks very unhappy.
Jamie Miss, he came over and started to spoil our game and was hitting me.

Such an opening statement as this by the supervisor is polite, and probably helps to keep Jamie calm. It also gives him the opportunity of giving his side of the story before the supervisor makes up her/his mind about what actually went on.

The supervisor could try to get corroborative evidence from other children. After first talking to Jamie himself, she/he could then approach friends of the antagonists.

Supervisor Mark, Tony and Alan (Jamie's friends), would you come here for a minute please? Can you tell me what is going on here. It looks like Jamie is picking on Daniel. Is that right?
Mark No, miss. It was Daniel who started it. He just came over and starting picking on Jamie, and Jamie got fed up and hit him back. It weren't Jamie's fault.

The supervisor now has more information to help her/him decide the next course of action.

However, a problem with talking to the friends of the children actually involved in an incident is that they are likely to be partisan. In this particular case, only Jamie's friends were on the scene to talk to the supervisor. This is not to say that their views are best ignored completely, rather that their biased nature would need to be taken into account.

Another tactic would be to try to talk to any other children who might have witnessed the events, in the hope of getting a more accurate description. It might also be useful to do this in a discreet way, especially if these other children are younger/weaker than the participants. Research suggests that a major reason why children are reticent about reporting incidents of bullying and other forms of misbehaviour that they witness is because they fear 'revenge' attacks from the pupils who bully.

INFORMATION BOX 6.4 INFORMATION ABOUT ROUGH-AND-TUMBLE PLAY

- Rough-and-tumble play is common in children of junior/middle school age. Overall it may take up about a tenth of their free play time on the playground.
- Rough-and-tumble play may be a feature of the play of all groups of children.
- There are marked individual and group differences in the extent to which children engage in rough-and-tumble play. Some children habitually engage in a lot of this form of play whereas others almost always refrain from participating. In general terms, boys tend to engage in more rough-and-tumble play than girls, and 7–8-year-olds more than than 11–12-year-olds.

  However, such group differences reflect general tendencies, and it would be unwise to make specific predictions about any given child's probable level of participation in rough-and-tumble play.
- Most junior school pupils can reliably distinguish between rough-and-tumble play and serious aggression in other pupils, but there may be a minority for whom this presents a problem.
- When asked why they engage in rough-and-tumble, the most common reason given by junior school pupils is 'because it is fun'.

There are several reasons why a supervisor may not be able to correctly identify bullying on the playground. Some examples might include:

- when a supervisor has not seen the whole situation;
- rough-and-tumble play might be confused with bullying/aggression;
- when a bullied pupil has been coerced into saying that she/he has not been bullied.

Hypothetical examples of each of these types of situation are described in **Information Boxes 6.3, 6.5** and **6.7** along with some suggestions about how best to deal with them.

A different reason why supervisors may find it difficult at times to correctly identify bullying on the playground is that some behaviours that look aggressive are actually playful as far as the participating children are concerned. Rough-and-tumble play is a category of children's playground behaviour that comes to mind in this respect. Basically, it consists of playful fighting and chasing. **Information Box 6.4** describes

INFORMATION BOX 6.5 PROBLEMS IN DISTINGUISHING BETWEEN ROUGH-AND-TUMBLE PLAY AND BULLYING

Case study

Jane and Carly (aged 10 years) both watched the same television programme last night and now enact scenes from this in their play. This involves mock fighting which is fairly vigorous. Jane wrestles Carly to the ground and sits on top of her and pretends to punch her about the face.

A playground supervisor sees this from a distance and assumes that it is a real fight. She rushes over and without stopping to enquire what is happening, drags Jane off and reports her to the head teacher for 'fighting'.

Jane argues that she was only playing, but the supervisor and head-teacher ignore this as an excuse.

Analysis and suggestions

The supervisor has made a snap decision about what was happening. In the first instance, she/he might have asked both pupils what they were doing in a calm and polite manner. If both girls had indicated that they were only playing a game, then the matter could have ended more or less there (or perhaps after the supervisor had pointed out that the girls might damage their clothes by playing on the ground, and that perhaps they might like to calm down slightly as they might hurt themselves).

A problem with presenting this tactic as the best solution to this type of problem is that on some occasions, a victim of actual bullying may be so frightened of getting the bully into trouble that she/he might agree with the bully that they were only playing. This point is discussed in more detail in **Information Box 6.6**.

some of what we know about the nature of rough-and-tumble play, **Information Box 6.5** describes a hypothetical example of how it may present a problem for a playground supervisor, and **Information Box 6.6** gives some suggestions for how an adult might more easily distinguish it from aggressive interactions.

Some pupils who bully are very good at disguising the nature of their relationship with their victims, and explicitly warn them prior to adult intervention, that they are to say that they are only playing. Again there is no easy or single way round this problem, but some suggestions are given in **Information Box 6.7**.

INFORMATION BOX 6.6   HOW TO DISTINGUISH BETWEEN ROUGH-AND-TUMBLE PLAY AND AGGRESSIVE/BULLYING BEHAVIOUR

Use as many of the cues as possible:

- **Facial and vocal expression** – rough-and-tumble play is often accompanied by smiling or laughing, and this 'play face' signals to other children that one's intentions are playful. By contrast, serious fighting is accompanied by frowns, staring, redness of face, grimacing and crying.
- **Outcome** – after rough-and-tumble play, children often stay together, whereas after a real fight they tend to move away from each other.
- **Self-handicapping** – in a playful fight, a child (especially one who is stronger or older) may allow another child to pin him or her during wrestling, or to catch him or her during chasing. This does not occur during serious fighting and chasing.
- **Restraint** – in playful fighting, a child will often not actually make contact with a touch or blow, or if contact is made it will be relatively gentle. In serious fighting, contact is not restrained and full force is often used.
- **Role reversals** – in playful fighting, partners deliberately take turns, such as being on top or underneath in wrestling, and chasing or being chased. Again, this does not usually happen in aggressive fighting.
- **Number of partners** – in playful fighting, it is common for many children to be involved, perhaps ten or more. Serious fights usually only involve two children at a time.
- **Onlookers** – playful fighting has little if any interest for non-participants. In contrast, serious fighting usually draws onlookers, and a crowd of children may congregate.

Prevention strategies

In our second training session with lunchtime supervisors, we discussed a number of specific strategies which may be used to prevent bullying. Some of these suggestions are given in this section. It is important to point out that these ideas are not intended solely for consumption by lunchtime supervisors, since they may be helpful to other members of a school's staff.

INFORMATION BOX 6.7   PROBLEMS IN IDENTIFYING BULLYING:
CHILDREN MAY BE TOO FRIGHTENED TO SAY THAT THEY ARE
ACTUALLY BEING BULLIED

Case study

A lunchtime supervisor sees what she/he thinks is a case of bullying.
She/he approaches the children and seeks clarification about what is going
on.

Supervisor   Karen, what are you doing to Susan? She doesn't look happy.

The supervisor has not actually accused Karen of bullying, but has made
it clear that she/he is aware that it is a possibility. The onus is now on
Karen to explain what is going on.

Karen   No, we're only playing, aren't we Susan?
Susan   Yes, we're only playing.

The supervisor is not convinced, partly because Susan does not seem
enthusiastic, and partly because Karen and Susan do not usually play
together.

Supervisor   I'm sorry to disturb your game, but I need to have a word with
               Susan about helping me. Can you come with me a minute
               Susan, I want you to take a message to Mrs X (another super-
               visor). Susan will be back in a minute Karen, is that OK?
               (Walks away with Susan).

The supervisor now has the opportunity to talk to Susan without Karen
being present. Either directly or in a more roundabout way, the supervisor
can ask Susan if she wants to rejoin the game with Karen, or if she would
prefer to play with someone else. If the incident with Karen was one that
Susan wished to withdraw from, but she was frightened to say so directly
and in front of Karen, she now has the opportunity of doing so in a way
that she knows will not make Karen angry with her. The supervisor must
decide whether she/he will approach Karen over the incident. In contrast, if
the incident was truly amicable, then Susan now has the chance of re-
joining Karen.

Another tactic, in this sort of situation, is to ask for details about the
game:

Supervisor   Karen, what are you doing to Susan? She doesn't seem happy.

Karen	No, we're only playing, aren't we Susan?
Susan	Yes, we're only playing.
Supervisor	What are you playing?
Karen	A game.
Supervisor	What game? I don't remember seeing this game before.
Karen	All different things.
Supervisor	Can you tell me what sort of things you are playing?
Karen	No, miss, I forget.
Supervisor	What about you, Susan, can you tell me what game you are playing?
Susan	No miss.

This sort of response might be an indication that all is not as Karen would have the supervisor believe. It might then be useful for the supervisor to have a word with Susan away from Karen, perhaps in the manner described above. Once Susan's point of view is known, the supervisor can take appropriate action, which might be to integrate Susan into a game with some other children and/or to tackle Karen over the incident.

Patrol 'bullying hot spots'

Many schools have locations in and around the playground where bullying is most likely to occur. This is probably because the location is hidden from general view, for example, behind mobile classrooms stationed in the playground, behind out-buildings such as bicycle sheds, and in toilets which can be entered from the playground.

Encourage supervisors to visit these locations on a regular basis, and be seen to do so by the pupils. In this way, children may be less inclined to bully in these more out of the way locations. Moreover, this patrolling strategy would also help ensure that all children had safe access to all legitimate locations in and around the playground.

Find out who is often involved in bullying

By being aware of individual children who are known to have engaged in bullying activities in the past, and those who have been picked on, the playground supervisor can keep an eye those pupils who may be likely to become involved in the future. However, labelling children should be avoided.

Avoid labelling children

It is very important to point out that information about which children have bullied other pupils and which have been picked on in the past should not be used to label children, either as 'bullies' or as 'victims', in any absolute sense. Children bully and get bullied for complex reasons, many of which appear to be related to specific events in their lives. It may be more helpful to think of children as being involved in problem behaviour rather than being problem children.

Labelling can also lead to erroneous conclusions about what a given child is doing. For example, a supervisor who perceives a child to be a bully may be more likely to misperceive her/his participation in rough-and-tumble play as aggressive than a supervisor who has not labelled the child in this way.

Watch out for lone pupils

Pupils who spend a lot of time on their own on the playground may be especially prone to bullying. The playground supervisor could be encouraged to be on the look out for lone pupils, and to take steps where it appears appropriate to integrate them into the playful activities of other pupils.

Talk to pupils who are directly involved

Talking to children who are known to have been involved in bullying problems in the past, reinforces the notion that adult supervisors are a feature of playground life. For children who may be prone to bullying, this may make them think twice about bullying in the future as they are made aware that they are known by the supervisor. For children who have been picked on in the past, it may engender a feeling of security or, even better, it may facilitate a relationship of trust that will make it easier for the child to report any instances of bullying that they experience in the future.

Make it known that bullying won't be tolerated

At every opportunity, the supervisor should reiterate the notion that bullying behaviour is not allowed and will be treated as a serious offence. Hence no child can use ignorance of the rules as an excuse.

Responding to aggression and resolving conflict

Aggression and bullying are likely to occur in most playgrounds at one time or another, despite our best efforts to prevent them. Consequently, it is important that adults are ready for such behaviour and have devised a system of responding. This section will describe a number of possible options. The general aim of these systems is to discourage certain forms of behaviour by implementing specific sanctions, that are known to all members of the school community, in a consistent manner. In no case can we recommend overly punitive measures. Whatever their form, these may be counter-productive given that children may imitate them, and they may give children the implicit impression that physical force is justified.

Try to keep calm

Some of the things children do or say can be very provoking, but it is counter-productive in many ways to show anger. For example, an aggressive response by an adult to misbehaviour by children may actually foster aggression and misbehaviour rather than discourage it, since children tend to imitate the behaviour of adults. Thus, adults may unwittingly be contributing to the causes of bullying and aggressive behaviour – those very things that are viewed as among the least acceptable forms of playground interaction. By staying calm, a playground supervisor can show to children that she/he is in control.

Avoid rushing

If an incident is spotted some distance away, a slow but deliberate walk over to the scene provides thinking time and lets the pupils know that something is about to happen.

Do not be seen to jump to conclusions

Calmly ask the participants and onlookers of a suspected incidence of bullying what was happening, but retain sufficient control to avoid a cacophony of individuals all talking at once. Ask a child by name, to explain things. Any other child who clearly wants to tell her/his side of the story can politely be asked to 'Wait a minute until X has finished'.

Listen well

Try to listen to what the children say, rather than pre-judging a situation. This also serves to show to the children that the supervisor is a fair person, and hence one that deserves respect.

Don't be side-tracked

Some children are adept are steering the conversation away from the issues at hand, especially if it relates to their own misbehaviour. The playground supervisor has the authority to disregard such attempts, and to keep to the point at hand. The 'broken record' technique may be useful in this respect (see Chapter 5), whereby the supervisor repeats a question several times if necessary in order to elicit an appropriate response from a child. If a child does try to change the subject, comments such as, 'That's all very well, but I want to know . . . ' are usually enough to show that the supervisor won't be side-tracked.

Avoid sarcasm and direct personal criticism

Children's self-esteem can be severely damaged by put-downs from adults. A major goal of playground supervision is to discourage unacceptable behaviour and/or deal with such instances that do arise, but to achieve these ends at the expense of lower-ing children's self-esteem is not, in our view, acceptable. Moreover, the tendency to use such cutting remarks may be copied by the children, resulting in more verbal bullying rather than less. It also may be the case that children with low self-esteem are those who are more likely to become involved in such behaviours as bullying, either as perpetrators or as those on the receiving end. In such cases, supervisors should look for ways to bolster the child's self-worth rather than reduce it even farther.

Label the behaviour and not the child

Children engage in bullying for a variety of reasons, sometimes as an (in)direct response to some negative event in their lives, and sometimes because they have themselves been bullied. For this reason, and others, it may be better to label the misbehaviour as bad rather than the child her/himself. Some children may actually try to live up to labels applied to them, and this does seem to apply to undesirable as well as desirable behaviour. Hence, 'Jason, that was an awful thing to do to David' is better than 'Jason, you are nothing but a bully'.

Don't make threats that can't or won't be carried out

It is sometimes tempting to threaten severe sanctions in the hope of getting children to do what they are told. If these threats cannot actually be carried out, or the adult is not actually prepared to enforce them, then her/his status is likely to be eroded. Children will quickly learn that an adult tends to make empty threats and so will be more difficult to control in the future.

Don't use severe threats at the very beginning

When directing children to do something, it is best not to begin with severe threats. The supervisor leaves nothing in reserve should the child not respond to her/his request. Thus, if a child did not respond to a request to 'pick your sweet paper up now or I will take you to the headteacher', then the most likely outcomes are all far from desirable:

- the supervisor takes the child to the headteacher, who is likely to view such action as inappropriate, or believe that the supervisor could have done something else to make the child pick up the litter;
- the supervisor could let the child off, but in doing so she/he will look weak and lacking in authority;
- the supervisor could impose a less severe sanction, which again undermines her/his status, and reinforces the child's view that the supervisor won't carry out what she/he threatens.

Avoid using teachers as a means of controlling children

As we have seen in an earlier section, lunchtime supervisors should enjoy the same level of authority as members of the teaching staff. However, threats such as, 'If you do that again, I'll tell your teacher' give the impression that the supervisor has a lower status than the teacher, and that misbehaviour is somehow made more serious when a teacher is informed.

Consider using a 'time out' tactic

Children sometimes become very agitated and angry during disputes on the play-ground. This may not be the best state in which the supervisor should try to deal with the situation. Giving the child time to calm down may make them more reasonable. The child could, for example, be asked to stand against a wall until the supervisor returns. Time out will also provide an opportunity to deal with any injured children without giving offenders the impression that they have 'got away with it' or that the supervisor cannot cope with the situation. 'Time out' should not last too long – a minute or two will be sufficient.

Look for a 'win win' solution

Like many adults, children often do not respond well to being backed into a corner, with no chance of putting their point of view across or no way out of the situation. A solution which is seen as acceptable both to the supervisor and to the child who has misbehaved, may be appropriate in some situations. For example, the supervisor may feel that a child's behaviour in spoiling another's game merited intervention, but not escalation to involve a senior manager. She/he could suggest, 'David, you know that sort of behaviour is not tolerated in this school, don't you? If you promise not to do it again and go and apologise to Simon and Paul, I won't say anything more. Is that OK with you?'

This sort of approach reinforces the view that the supervisor is fair-minded and reasonable, and may foster such traits in the children she/he supervises.

Develop a hierarchy of sanctions

In general terms, children appear to benefit from having a clear hierarchy of sanctions. This might begin with a discussion of acceptable and unacceptable behaviour, verbal warnings for first and/or minor offences, involvement of senior management for subsequent and/or serious offences, contact with parents if the misbehaviour persists, and eventually exclusion from the playground for a specified period. Such a structured approach may help a child develop a sense of severity of misbehaviour.

Yellow and red card system

A specific example of an approach that employs a hierarchy of sanctions is the yellow and red card system, recommended by Imich and Jefferies (1989), and described by Blatchford (1989). The following description is based on those articles but with some relatively minor revisions. The system is based on sanctions imposed in soccer and other sports. For relatively minor offences, such as shouting, the individual is put on 'time out' in which they are instructed to stand for a brief period, say 5 minutes, at the edge of the playground where they are not allowed to talk with other pupils. For more serious offences, such as bullying and racist remarks, the individual is shown a yellow card which is clearly understood by both pupils and members of the school's staff to indicate that something serious has occurred. The child's name is written on the yellow card and in order for the card to be destroyed the child must have the card signed by one of the playground supervisors at the end of the lunch break on five separate occasions. Only good behaviour is sufficient reason for a supervisor to sign the card. If a child is shown another yellow card while the first is still in operation, then she/he must obtain signatures for ten separate days of good behaviour. Finally, if a child shows another serious offence while two yellow cards are in operation, then the child is automatically shown a red card. This results in total exclusion from the playground at lunchtime for a specified period.

The advantages of such an approach to managing misbehaviour are that it provides a graded system of responding in which children clearly know what the consequences of certain acts will be, as well as what will happen if they persist in acting in ways that they know are unacceptable. The fact that a red card leads to automatic exclusion from the playground means that parents will have to find alternative childcare arrangements, and hence parents may be more likely to extol good behaviour in their children.

Encourage positive behaviour

Given that lunchtime supervisors are in daily contact with the children in the playground, they are in a very favourable position to encourage good behaviour. As we have seen, there are good reasons why schools need to consider ways of discouraging negative behaviour such as bullying, and devising ways of responding when it does occur. Nevertheless, there are equally good reasons why schools should try to encourage positive behaviour. At the very least, a child who is behaving well is not behaving badly. Moreover, schools are in the business of not only enhancing children's intellects but also their development into responsible citizens. In this section, some suggestions for facilitating positive behaviour will be presented.

Adopt a 'catch them being good' philosophy

Rather than merely being on the look out for instances of bad behaviour, be sensitive to good behaviour. When children do behave in an exemplary manner, they should be rewarded in some way (see below). By responding to good as well as bad behaviour, the supervisor will come to be perceived as someone who is fair-minded and not simply someone who is performing a negative policing role on the playground. Moreover, children who often misbehave as a way of getting attention from an adult can be encouraged to be well-behaved as an alternative and more attractive way of receiving the attention.

Small rewards can be effective

A smile or a nod can be a powerful reinforcer of good behaviour, especially if the supervisor is well-respected by the pupils. There is also evidence to suggest that verbal praise can be especially helpful in this respect. Comments such as, 'Tony, I must say you've played very well today. I noticed you taking turns with the younger boys. Well done' encourage children to repeat the behaviour.

Have the same reward system as teaching staff

For cases of exceptionally good behaviour, the supervisor should be in a position to use the same rewards as a class teacher. For example, if a child has stepped in to stop another child from bullying a smaller pupil, and has done so in a sensible way by bringing the offender to the supervisor and explaining what has happened, then the child's good behaviour should be rewarded in the same way that good academic performance is rewarded by the teacher in class.

Lunchtime supervisors and teachers could meet to discuss the sorts of playground behaviours that should merit such highly valued rewards.

Pass on information about good behaviour

Playground supervisors can inform a child's class teacher that she/he has behaved well that lunchtime. The supervisor should do this loudly and in front of pupils. Again, this tactic reinforces the idea that adults are not merely interested in misbehaviour, but are just as concerned with good behaviour. Similarly, it emphasises that behaviour in both the classroom and the playground are viewed as important.

Remember individual differences

Whereas some children almost always play co-operatively in the playground, others are more likely to misbehave. Look out for cases in which the latter do play well with their peers, and deliberately reinforce this behaviour. This is not to say that generally well-behaved children should be overlooked. On the contrary, the supervisor should intermittently show her/his approval of the child's good behaviour. However, the beneficial effect of showing approval may be diminished if it is used too freely or is given without due merit.

Respond to children's self-reports of good behaviour

Children who find it difficult to avoid misbehaving sometimes seek approval for instances of their own good behaviour. They are often accompanied by their friends who are prepared to endorse what has been said. Respond to these requests in a positive manner, as this will reinforce the good behaviour and show to the child that they can get peer-status from behaving well. Supervisors should resist the temptation to show disbelief or say sarcastic things like 'That makes a change' or 'What are you after?'

Introduce a pupil 'Things I am proud of' book

Class teachers encourage children to make their own 'Things I am proud of' book or file. On a regular basis, each pupil spends some time either writing or drawing the things that they did during play or the lunch break which they feel proud of. The class teacher should give positive feedback to pupils for this activity in the same way as for academic success.

Set up pupil self-monitoring

The class teacher guides the children in an activity designed to measure their own behaviour on the playground. They could be encouraged to make a record sheet on which they record how they felt about their own behaviour in the playground. For younger pupils, and to save time with older pupils, a Smiley face system could be used. The class teacher should monitor the record sheets, to show that she/he is interested in what happens on the playground, and she/he should respond with positive reinforcement where appropriate.

Improving the quality of play

Pupils often wander aimlessly about the playground, often complaining of being bored. Some teachers and parents have also complained that many children have lost the ability to engage in co-operative and friendly play with their peers, and that traditional games are disappearing. While this may be an exaggeration to some extent, there does appear to be a case for adults trying to improve the quality of children's play, and this section will consider some possibilities. However, my own impression is that it would not be appropriate for adults to take over playtime to the extent that they dictate children's activities. There is evidence that children gain many benefits from playing in ways that they choose for themselves and without close adult supervision. Our role, therefore, should perhaps be to encourage them to play in more satisfactory and/or enjoyable ways without appearing to be too dictatorial.

Providing playground equipment

In some schools, especially where children come from impoverished backgrounds, there may be little opportunity for play with small pieces of equipment. You may like to consider providing pupils with equipment, such as skipping ropes, hoops, footballs and tennis balls, inflatable beach balls and soft foam balls. These can be highly attractive to many pupils; they are ideal from a safety point of view, and are not very costly.

Admittedly, providing equipment may mean extra work for some members of staff in handing out and collecting items, as well as monitoring the way it is being used. You should also consider how to ensure that items of equipment are not 'lost' – a basic logging in–out system might help in this respect. This extra effort could be more than compensated for in the reduction of boredom-related misdemeanours.

Teaching games in class

Devote some lessons to teaching pupils how to play specific games on the playground. You could use examples from their own childhood, from published sources and/or encourage children to share their own ideas for games. Older children could also be invited to come into classes of younger pupils to teach them some of the games that they enjoy.

Establishing a games library

In small groups of three or four, ask pupils to decide on a game that they will, at a specified time, communicate to the rest of the class. They may need to do some research, and to discuss the project with their teacher. They may wish to communicate the game orally, by means of pictures/diagrams that they have drawn, or even by acting out the game to the rest of the class. The groups are then asked to find a way of recording the details of the game for the school's games library. Again, this could be a verbal description on an audio tape, a pictorial representation with instructions in a book or file, or even a video record of the children actually playing the game. Once the games library is set up, all children in the school are given access to it.

Improving the quality of wet playtimes

A consistent complaint from lunchtime supervisors and teachers alike is that when children are forced to spend playtime inside school because of bad weather, even more problems than normal tend to arise. Children are deprived of the chance to 'let off steam', they often have very little to occupy them and they often spend time in the classroom without the constant presence of an adult. Here we present some relatively simple suggestions that may help.

Theme activity rooms

Agree on a number of different types of activities which will be catered for during wet playtimes. You could include an active games area in the hall for such things as leapfrog, running activities or a disco; a passive games area for such things as snakes and ladders, a video room and a quiet reading area. Some of the older more responsible pupils could be asked to supervise some of the younger pupils, perhaps by reading them a story or showing them how to use the school's computer. This latter tactic could free some of the lunchtime supervisors to patrol the different locations where the children are spending the wet lunchtime.

Provide more materials/equipment

Although many schools are facing financial problems, spending money on such things as board games and modelling materials could be a good investment if it helps to reduce the amount of problem behaviour during wet playtimes. Pupils who are about to go on to secondary school could be asked to donate any such games and materials to the school they are leaving. Each class could have a box of ready prepared 'wet play' activities.

SUMMARY

This chapter has outlined numerous suggestions for helping reduce playground bullying. Some of these ideas may have the added bonus of helping reduce other undesirable behaviour and/or encouraging good behaviour. Some of the suggestions are quite simple to implement (such as introducing lunchtime supervisors to pupils) whereas others involve a lot more time and effort (such as training lunchtime supervisors). It is acknowledged that you may be unable to put all of our suggestions into practice for several reasons. Playground bullying is understandably not the only issue high on schools' agendas, and even if it was, some schools may be attracted to other approaches described in the various chapters of this book. Moreover, some of the suggestions may not appeal to everybody.

It may be helpful if you view the many suggestions contained in this chapter as a menu from which you can select as many or as few items as you wish. Realistically, the great pressures you face in school at the moment might mean that you will prefer to gradually introduce the various options, working at a pace suited to your own individual requirements and resources.

Whatever you decide, it is clear that playground bullying is a problem that won't go away on its own. Some action is surely called for, even if it is not all that you would like.

how to improve the school ground environment as an anti-bullying strategy

CATHERINE HIGGINS

The school ground environment and bullying

This section is about how to improve your school grounds as part of an anti-bullying strategy. Research has shown a strong correlation between bullying and poor playground environments. Bullying won't disappear if the playground environment alone is improved but, equally, any number of interventions may be used to little effect if the physical environment does not support 'positive' play.

A strategy for improving your grounds is set out below and participatory methods for the whole school to use are illustrated. These are aimed at junior and primary schools but many processes and ideas can be modified for secondary school use. School ground improvements should be closely linked to other interventions such as lunchtime supervisor training.

First, let's establish what we mean by poor playground environments and their potential effects on bullying behaviour.

Does your school have a poor playground environment?

The response to this question may be painfully obvious and a definite 'YES!' One way to make the answer clear is to compare the playground with inside the school building.

Your classrooms are likely to be highly stimulating, warm, colourful, diverse environments. There will probably be pupils' pictures on the wall, lots to look at and do, and niches for different activities. This may be in sharp contrast to outside. At worst junior and primary school grounds consist of one or two small bleak bare asphalt yards; the only features perhaps a hopscotch floor painting or football area and a small patch of worn, muddy grass. Your school may have playing fields and perhaps some trees. Even with this extra greenery and space the environment may be similarly featureless with little that encourages positive and varied outdoor uses.

- **A poor environment is one that lacks diversity and stimulation and offers few settings for a variety of educational, social, physical and creative activities.**

Teachers are now very much aware that 'tarmac prisons' are no longer acceptable. Let's look at some of the effects this type of environment can have on bullying behaviour.

What effects can a poor school ground environment have on bullying behaviour?

As a teacher or lunchtime supervisor you will almost certainly have observed in children the effects of poor school ground environments. You may have witnessed or experienced all or some of the following:

Boredom

With little to stimulate children's interest dull environments can favour anti-social activities. Bored children may, for stimulation, or out of frustration

- pick fights,
- tease,
- bully.

Crowding

The playground – one featureless unstructured space – is supposed to cater for many play activities but is in reality a good resource for few. Children are crowded onto a noisy 'free for all' pitch; a frightening, intimidating, confusing place especially for younger children. Conflicts, arguments and injuries inevitably occur as children compete for space and paltry resources, or fly about in unrestrained frenzied chasing and running games.

Marginalisation

Older boys tend to dominate the playground with vigorous football games. These can forcibly marginalise other pupils (often girls and younger children) and their activities. Because there is no provision or protection for less vigorous or spatially demanding play the message can seem to be: if you are older, physically stronger *and* can play football then the playground belongs to you. This does nothing to encourage a co-operative caring attitude among pupils.

Exclusion

Playgrounds are commonly seen and used by children as proving grounds which establish power relationships. A playground that is good for active running games (notably football) but poor for many others reinforces certain social relationships. Those who do not excel in skills required for dominant games are noticeably excluded because they have little opportunity to engage in other (solitary) activities. Victims of bullying are frequently those who appear different from their peers. If being 'normal' means the ability to play football or a particular game then those who cannot or do not may be prone to bullying. We have all seen how poorly 'loners' and the less active and physically strong fare in the playground.

Low self-esteem

Low self-esteem can precipitate bullying behaviour. The evaluation system in schools may engender a sense of failure in some children. The impoverished playground environment can reinforce the negative effects of academic assessment because it provides few opportunities for children who do not excel in class to achieve through varied outdoor activities.

Difficult supervision

Many playgrounds are hard if not impossible to supervise well. As we have seen elsewhere dealing with bullying incidents effectively is crucial to changing behaviour. On a daily basis supervisors have to deal with the combined effects of boredom, crowding, marginalisation, exclusion and low self-esteem noted above.

School ethos

School ethos (the 'atmosphere' in a school) must surely be affected by a barren harsh external environment that often looks more like a prison exercise yard than a place for children. Inhospitable places do little to encourage a sense of pride and belonging for teachers, pupils, lunchtime supervisors and parents. Bleak school yards do nothing to suggest that school is a caring environment. Bullying, as we have seen, thrives in an 'unsupportive atmosphere'.

So, what makes a positive school ground?

What is a good school ground environment?

Playgrounds should not be indifferent or 'negative' places but ones that children and (through them) adults love. School grounds have huge potential as resources for teaching and play as witness the many schools who have already made environmental changes. These changes have often emphasised teaching functions (e.g. wildlife gardens or ponds for nature study) rather than being broad-based improvements for play or social activities. As we shall see, if we are to influence bullying and foster more equal relations and social interactions by providing a more 'supportive' environment we need to treat the playground holistically.

The environment we are aiming to create should be rich, diverse, flexible and multi-functioning, with settings, areas and features for the fullest range of play experience and teaching functions. It should be a place full of greenery, colour and texture but one which is also secure, safe and easily supervised and can be maintained. It must above all be an environment which allows direct involvement of pupils both during construction and after.

Pupil participation in the process of change we believe is vital to the success of improvements and maximises benefits as a bullying intervention. We shall look at this in more detail later.

What effects can improving the school grounds have on bullying behaviour?

With active participation of pupils an improved playground environment can have several benefits, many of which will help to influence levels of bullying. These are shown in **Information Box 7.1**.

INFORMATION BOX 7.1 BENEFITS OF PUPIL PARTICIPATION IN PLAYGROUND IMPROVEMENTS

- Improved status and confidence
- Reduced playground aggression and squabbling
- Increased imaginative play
- Improved social and motor skills
- Improved relationships and communication between pupils, teachers and non-teaching staff
- Less boredom

How to improve the school ground environment

The process of changing the school grounds can be divided into six main phases (**Information Box 7.2**). We think it is important to follow these to gain maximum benefit from the process as well as the end results. If you are only able to tackle part of the playground the process can be adapted for one area.

These stages have been developed for use with or without the involvement of a landscape designer (see below). They are based on stages of a process that landscape designers are often trained to use and on specially developed participatory techniques.

Before we describe each of these stages it is important to establish the meaning of participatory design versus 'traditional' design and the relevance of this to changing bullying behaviour.

The importance of participatory design and implementation for bullying intervention

Participatory design means that users of a product (in our case the school grounds) create the designs for it. This is in contrast to a more common system where we entrust the design and implementation (of a product) to a professional or specialist.

The benefits of participatory changes were illustrated above and we strongly recommend that participation is an integral part of your playground improvements. Ideally the whole school should be involved throughout. The communication and sharing of ideas cultivates an atmosphere of understanding and co-operation and a feeling amongst children that their needs and ideas are being taken seriously. Thinking and talking about their playground and behaviour allows children to

---

INFORMATION BOX 7.2   STAGES FOR IMPROVING THE SCHOOL
GROUNDS

1 Getting started
2 Information gathering
3 Goal-setting: deciding what changes should be made
4 Creating designs
5 Implementing the designs
6 Maintenance and review

---

consider their power relationships within that environment. These factors can in turn
help with the implementation and setting up of other bullying interventions and
policies.

- **The *way the playground is changed* – *the
  participation process* – is as important as the end result.**

Let's follow this process stage by stage.

Stage 1 Getting started

The decision to improve your playground will be the easiest part of the process! The
idea may come from the headteacher, a teacher, non-teaching staff, parent, governor
or from the pupils themselves.

Who is going to help?

The first thing to establish is who is going to be involved in the changes. All of the
following can contribute to the project:

Landscape designer

Decide early on whether you are going to use professional help from a landscape
designer. A good designer can help to create a school ground which meets all the
needs and desires of users. They are normally trained to see the potential of a site and
to resolve conflicts of use; creating designs which provide for people as well as nature.
They will help you make the most of your site as well as give technical advice on

plants and structures. They also work closely with other specialists, e.g. artists or conservationists. In this case you will also require that the landscape designer has experience of working on participatory design projects.

Often the deciding factor in whether to use a designer is financial. You may be lucky enough to have a local authority landscape architect, CTAC, Groundwork Trust or CLAWS worker whose services may be free or subsidised. In many cases using a landscape designer will not be an option, but if you can afford it, it will be money well spent.

Pupils

The importance of children's involvement has already been stressed.

Teaching staff

It is likely that all staff will be keen to change the grounds. Some will be more enthusiastic and have more time to give than others.

Co-ordinator

You may find it easiest to designate one teacher as project organiser or co-ordinator. This individual ideally needs spare time from teaching commitments as the amount of hours the role can take up should not be underestimated.

Non-teaching staff

Lunchtime supervisors and caretakers will need to be involved if changes are to be successful and not resented.

School Governors

The project will need the approval and support of school governors.

Parents and PTA

Parents often have a huge amount of skill, resources and commitment to offer playground improvement projects. If you do not have funds allocated for improvements a parent or the PTA may take responsibility for raising money.

LEA and Local Authority

Your local council may provide information and resources.

Local voluntary organisations and individuals

These may include conservation volunteers, wildlife groups, community arts organisations.

Students from other educational establishments

Students from secondary schools and tertiary education, e.g. art students.

Funding and grant-making bodies

Local firms, the Tree Council, the Countryside Commission, etc. are possible sources of funds.

Organisation

Each school will have different ways of organising to get things off the ground and encourage support: meetings, newsletters, informal chatting. You should try to draw in as many people as possible (not forgetting the children) from the beginning so that a large body of resources and skills can be utilised to the fullest. However, it is important not to raise hopes too rapidly and risk disillusionment as things take time to achieve:

INFORMATION BOX 7.3   GETTING STARTED – THINGS TO REMEMBER

- Don't expect instant results – think in a timescale of years not months.
- Do expect to do a lot of fundraising – changing the grounds costs money!
- Do expect a time-consuming (but rewarding) process.
- Do expect to work hard to keep the momentum going.
- Do establish at this stage a good organisational and support structure.
- Do establish how the new environment can be maintained.

Stage 2   Information gathering

The next stage, once you have mobilised, is to gather as much information as possible about the 'existing situation'. You will need two main types: data about the physical site – so that how you might change it can be assessed; and information about the people (children, teachers, lunchtime supervisors) who use it – so that you can work out what sort of improvements will meet everyone's needs.

Gathering data on the physical site

It is useful to begin by getting hold of a large-scale (1:500 or larger) plan of the grounds. This may be available from the LEA or planning department of your local authority. If a smaller-scale plan is the only one available then you can enlarge it on a photocopier. Alternatively, you can organise a project in which pupils measure and make a sealed plan of the grounds. This 'base plan' is useful for recording information and will also be required later on for design and implementation. You should keep an original from which you can make as many copies as you require.

You will need to gather information about the physical aspects of the site (see **Information Box 7.4**).

This data can be gathered and recorded by pupils in many different forms as part of

---

INFORMATION BOX 7.4   PHYSICAL INFORMATION REQUIRED

- **Vegetation**   species, condition, size, wildlife habitats/food plants
- **Site drainage**   direction surface water drains to, poorly drained areas
- **Topography**   spot heights, level changes, slopes, flat areas, retaining walls
- **Microclimate**   sunny and shady areas, windy spots, sheltered areas, prevailing winds
- **Underground services**   pipes, drains and cables, (gas, electricity, water)
- **Structures**   walls and fences, buildings, other structures (materials and condition)
- **Surfacing**   e.g. grass, concrete, tarmac, paving slabs, soil
- **Soil**   type, quality, pH
- **Wildlife**   habitats, vertebrates, invertebrates
- **Boundaries**   type, materials, height, condition
- **Pollution**   air, noise, visual

curricular activities. For further information on methods and ways to record see *The outdoor classroom*, DES (now DFE) and Learning through Landscapes publications.

The information about your school site should be made into displays for the whole school to see. The data will be used later to help you identify positive resources of the site, e.g. existing trees, walls for murals, slopes for play features and negative attributes which detract from enjoyment of the site, e.g. exposed windy areas, noise from traffic.

Finding out about who uses the school ground and how they use it

It is important to find out about how children and staff are using and perceive the grounds before they are changed. Here we describe several popular methods which we have found successful for gathering this information and involving children. They were developed and adapted for schools' use by Lyndal Sheat from a variety of sources. We encourage you to try all or some of these. The method, purpose and limitations of each are explained in **Activity Boxes 7.1–7.4**.

ACTIVITY BOX 7.1   GIANT MAP

Purpose

The purpose of this exercise is to reveal how pupils and staff (yes, you can try it too!) perceive their school ground environment, interact with it and with each other in it. The Giant Map can tell us what aspects are valued or disliked, and about conflicts which exist between present uses and users (girls and boys, teachers and pupils, etc.) by recording information in plan form and stimulating discussion about what's there? who benefits? what sort of games happen? The map-making exercise starts the process of thinking about the school grounds and the sharing of ideas paves the way for consideration of how to make changes.

Method

Small groups (7–10) of children are asked to draw a giant map of their school grounds on a base plan which already shows the building(s) and boundaries of the site. The role of the facilitator is to encourage children to include every feature but not to suggest or prompt any elements. Whilst the maps are being created verbal exchanges such as activities, likes and dislikes,

---

shape, sizes and position of elements, conflicts in use are noted by the facilitator.

Limitations

A limiting factor in the use of this technique is the difficulty children (especially younger ones) have with producing 'conventional' maps. Objects are shown side on rather than in bird's eye view.

There is also the problematic tendency for a sub-group or individual to dominate the drawing of features on the giant map. As with all group techniques this must be controlled by the facilitator.

Interpretation

Interpreting information that is given can be difficult but you can be pretty certain that activities children enjoy and the features involved will be recorded in detail whilst others that are less important will be omitted or notionally shown.

A striking aspect of many maps in our project was the intense precision with which football areas/pitches were shown. Not only were the lines of the pitch drawn accurately but the individual players drawn with such care. **Figure 7.1**. shows an example of a Giant Map where this is apparent.

Children can interpret their own and each other's drawings.

ACTIVITY BOX 7.2 PHOTO SAFARI

Purpose

The purpose of the exercise is, as with the Giant Map, to gather information on perceptions and use of the existing environment. The form of the exercise enables children to work co-operatively and control decision-making.

Method

The method involves the use of a (disposable) camera. Small groups (five to eight) of children are asked to take a non-staff adult on a guided tour of the playground. Whilst doing so they are required to take pictures of features they like and dislike. Guidance is given on how to use the camera but children decide by group consensus what should be photographed. Pupils take it in turns to use the camera. Discussion throughout the tour plays an important part in revealing pupil's attitudes and can be recorded by the adult.

Interpretation

The photographs are processed quickly and a collage made which locates views on a map. Negative and positive images are identified with reproduced comments and quotations from pupils that have been recorded on the safari. This can be used in the next stage.

ACTIVITY BOX 7.3   A DAY IN THE LIFE OF ... ACTIVITIES CHART

Purpose

The purpose of this exercise is to encourage the pupils to think about and record their activities (outside of the classroom) through the day. This information will be useful when deciding what new elements need to be provided in the playground as it identifies activities enjoyed and how the present environment limits or provides for diverse play.

Method

The method requires groups of children to record their activities on a large chart which is divided into parts of the day: before school, at morning break, lunchtime, afternoon break and after school. The teacher's role is to stimulate discussion and make sure that all activities are recorded. **Figure 7.2.** shows an example of an activities chart.

ACTIVITY BOX 7.4   QUESTIONNAIRES

Purpose

Questionnaires can complement and influence analysis of other material gathered in group processes. They also allow quieter individuals the opportunity to convey information that may be lost in a group situation.

Method

Simple questionnaires can be devised, administered and answered by both pupils and staff to gather information. You may like to ask questions about the following:

- favourite playtime activities,
- favourite playground places,
- least liked aspects of playtime/playground,
- who the respondent likes to play with,
- does the respondent like or dislike their playground?

Interpretation

The method provides statistical results which you can display as bar charts or in other pictorial form. Age and gender differences can be assessed.

Other methods

There are many other ways to gather information including taped interviews. You may invent your own. Make sure that everyone has their say and that teaching staff, lunch time supervisors and the caretaker in particular are consulted. Participation is the key.

Stage 3   Goal-Setting – deciding what changes should be made

Evaluating and discussing information

Once information has been gathered it can be displayed in the school and form the focus of class discussion. Some information such as 'a day in the life of' charts can be

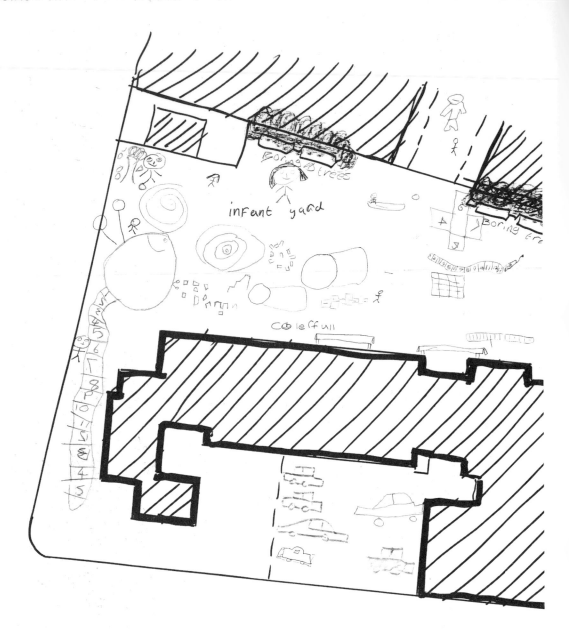

Figure 7.1 A giant map

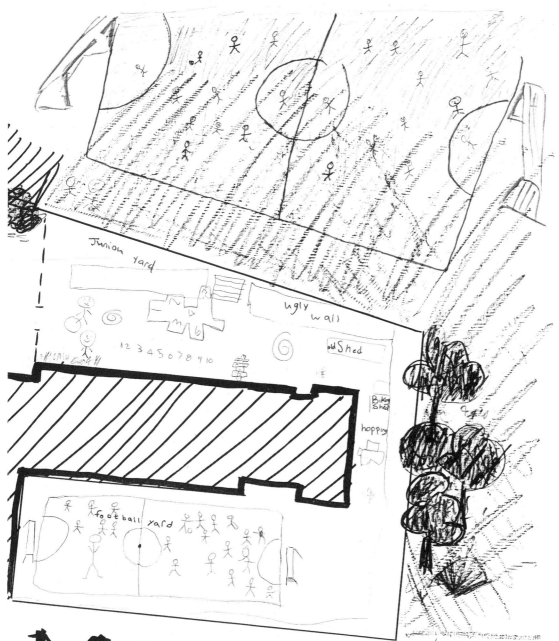

MAP

displayed as they are. Others such as 'photo safari' will need to be 'collaged'. The physical survey can be summarised on simple plans or diagrams.

Discussion should enable each class and the whole school to identify and crystallise a shared picture of the problems and potential of the school grounds and their use. You may like to focus your discussion around making two lists (see **Activity Box 7.5**).

Staff discussion

Teachers and lunchtime supervisors and can hold their own discussions and will have their particular concerns and observations.

Goal-setting

Having discussed the present situation and become more aware of what happens and what is liked and disliked in the playground it is possible to set goals for changing the environment.

ACTIVITY BOX 7.5   GOOD AND BAD THINGS ABOUT THE PLAY-GROUND

Bad things

- 'Football spoils some children's games.'
- 'There's not enough to do at play time.'
- 'Little ones are always getting knocked down.'
- 'Fights start in the playground if . . .'
- 'Tarmac hurts if you fall down.'
- 'We're always told not to play on the grass.'
- 'Mud gets everywhere.'
- 'The playground's very windy in winter.'
- 'There's too much noise to talk . . .'

Good things

- 'The playground is great for football.'
- 'We like to climb the trees.'
- 'We like going on the grass.'
- 'Behind the toilets is a good place for chatting with your friends.'
- 'Some children think . . .'

Goal-setting is a process of making decisions about what is desired and what it is possible to create for the new environment. It should be participatory and seek consensus (amongst teachers, pupils, lunchtime supervisors, governors) about which improvements should be made.

Goal setting is made up of two main processes: first, *idealism and idea generation* – i.e. 'brainstorming' of as many different imaginative ideas for the grounds as possible; and, second, *realism and consensus* – discussion and decision-making based on realistic options.

To foster both, several participatory techniques have been developed by Sheat from others. Two are described in **Activity Boxes 7.6 and 7.7** for you to try.

Ideas from other environments

A way to help stimulate ideas for the new environment is to visit schools which have made changes to their grounds or hold a slide show or cut pictures from magazines of types of environments that could be used.

Teachers' and lunchtime supervisors' goal-setting

Goal-setting with teaching staff can be implemented as an informal discussion session perhaps utilising information from pupils' exercises.

ACTIVITY BOX 7.6   CUE CARDS

This exercise involves discussion by groups of pupils using a previously prepared set of 'cue cards'. Each card has an image of an element that might form part of the new playground environment e.g. seats, trees, hiding places, pond. These can be gleaned from information revealed in ideal school drawings (see below) or by looking at other schools' ideas. **Figure 7.3** shows examples of some 'cue cards'. The group must decide by 'voting' on which elements they would like to have in their playground and which should be excluded. The features can then be graded from most popular to least popular according to how many of the group(s) voted for or against.

   Discussion during the cue cards exercise can reveal remarkably mature responses and an understanding of each other's requirements such as choosing items for younger age groups or suggesting ways to separate football from other play. The democratic debate and decision-making as a group enables realistic and popular choices to be made.

Figure 7.2 Example of an activities chart

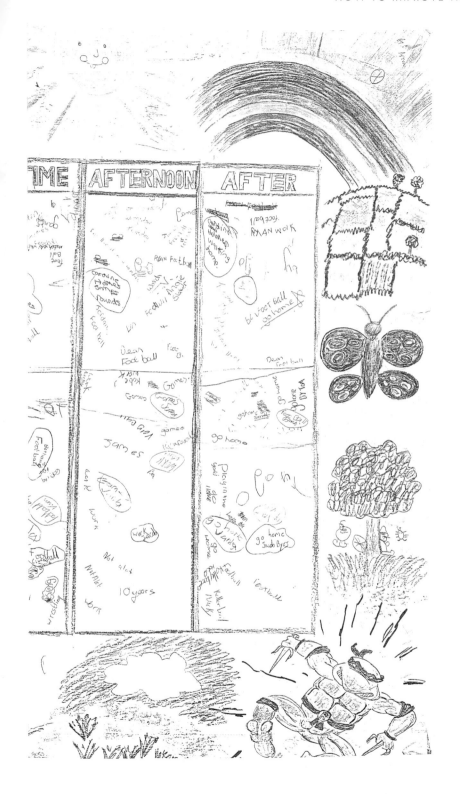

ACTIVITY BOX 7.7 IDEAL PLAYGROUND DRAWING

This exercise is very simple and commonly used for many purposes. Pupils are asked to draw a picture of their ideal school playground. They should be encouraged by teachers to include whatever they like however fantastic or unrealistic this might be. Many drawings may thus resemble funfairs or adventure playgrounds with death slides and helter-skelters. The purpose is to generate as many ideas as possible. Subsequent discussion can decide on the possibilities.

A simple analysis of popular features can be carried out by counting the number of times elements and items feature in children's drawings. The drawings reflect both children's *expectations* and their *experience*. Drawings can also be analysed to discover age and gender differences and similarities.

Although many items illustrated are obviously impractical the drawings produced by children should be taken as a serious indication of the types of activities they enjoy or are interested in. The drawings should therefore influence decisions about what to include in the new playground.

Goals for the new school ground environment

All the ideas from the whole school can be pooled and converted to a list of goals for the grounds. These will probably fall into two main categories. The first will be overall or general goals (aims) for the whole school ground. These set out the purpose and function of improvements, the 'philosophy' for making changes; the *type* of environment the school wants to have (**Information Box 7.5**), and the second will be site-specific features (**Information Box 7.6**).

Goals must be realistic (achievable). They must recognise conflicts of use and preference and accommodate as many pupils' and staff's ideas as possible.

Checklist of key issues to consider before making a design

At this stage you may choose to use a landscape designer to help you evolve a design from your goals. Whether you are able to or not we have listed below issues which will influence your design and should be considered before proceeding.

Diversity

The school ground design should provide, in appearance and function, as much diversity as possible for play, social, educational, visual and other sensory experiences. It

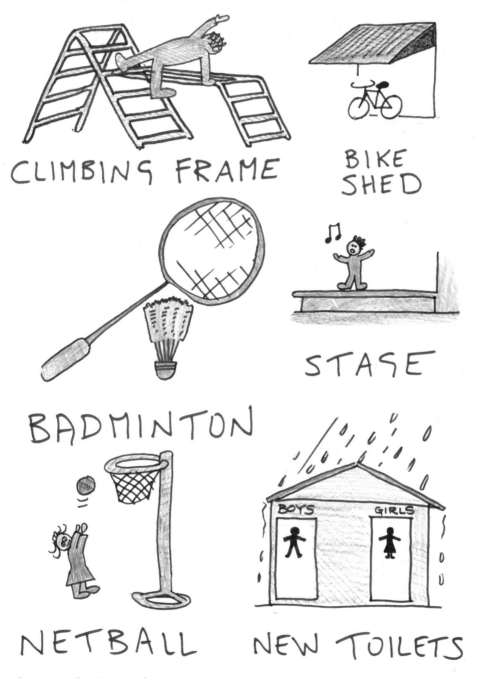

Figure 7.3 Cue cards

INFORMATION BOX 7.5   EXAMPLES OF GENERAL GOALS

- To improve the school ground resource by providing as many play and educational opportunities as possible. To use construction, planting, management, painting and landform to achieve this and thereby . . .
- enhance the grounds for nature study and curricular activities and provide settings and features for social, creative, physical, intellectual and solitary play.
- To zone the school grounds to provide for all these different new uses and thus reduce conflict.
- To improve safety and security of the school grounds.
- To increase 'greenery' and colour.
- To improve conditions for successful supervision.
- To create an environment that it will be possible to maintain.

---

should stimulate active *and* passive activities, and group and solitary play. There should be sequence and reflections of changing seasons or light. A variety of colours and textures, shape and size of spaces is important.

Flexibility

The school ground design should be flexible in several senses. Environments are dynamic and should:

- provide opportunity for manipulation, imaginative interpretation and changing use by children and teachers; everything constructed or planted in the playground should have several functions; expensive single function play structures may be inappropriate;
- be capable of being modified if things 'don't work', or (be capable of) being improved upon if new needs arise;
- allow for change through growth and management of vegetation and repair.

Child-scale

School ground designs must be child-scale. Paths can be narrower, steps shallower, seats, walls, fences and hedges lower (than those adults would create for themselves).Smaller children use spaces that are minuscule or even not apparent to adults. We understand this discrepancy forcefully if we return as adults to a childhood environment and are struck by its miniature appearance which contrasts strongly with our memory of the place.

INFORMATION BOX 7.6 EXAMPLES OF SITE-SPECIFIC FEATURES AND PLACES AS GOALS

Provision of:

- Seating, seating areas and 'quiet areas'
- Nature study gardens and features including pond
- Murals
- Play trails
- Play structures for climbing, balancing, and adventurous and imaginative play including use of timber structures, logs, tyres, rocks, landform and tunnels
- Trees, shrubs and flowers
- Enhanced sports facilities and areas (well separated from other zones)
- Play buildings and huts
- Growing areas for pupils

Children's sense of aesthetics

Much thought should be directed towards creating sensory stimulation specifically for children. Adults' sense of aesthetics can differ vastly from children's. Children may be said to have a more holistic sensory experience involving all the senses. Touch is particularly important to children so we should pay attention to the detail of texture in e.g. paving and walls, and in foliage and timber. Opportunities for imaginative play should be provided throughout the playground.

Safety

Decide how issues of safety will be dealt with. Each school must make their own checks on standards and bear responsibility for consulting the LEA and/or central government. Safety surfacing, heights of structures' materials, coatings, creosote and herbicides should all be checked.

Opportunities for pupil participation

Ideally designs for school grounds should incorporate structures, planting and art works that pupils can design and construct or carry out and manage. You can make a checklist of things children are capable of and to try to ensure that designs incorporate opportunities for them to design, build and plant.

- **The playground should be diverse, flexible, child-scale, and safe and should enable participation during and after construction.**

Limiting factors to consider

Some typical factors that limit improvements are considered below.

Funding and material resources

Many schools struggle financially. Environmental improvements compete with other projects for limited finance and resources. It is often the case that all costs must be met through fund-raising events, grants and donations.

You can adopt a strategy for fund-raising, phase improvements and explore the use of recycled, second-hand and donated materials.

Slow progress and lack of human resources

Far from being a limitation in a school grounds project, voluntary labour is often the driving force with superb skills, commitment and enthusiasm to offer. One of the main advantages of using voluntary labour (including pupils) is that the participation process with its attendant benefits is strongly continued. But teachers, parents, children, school governors and volunteers all have limited time to give to an improvement project. Improvements will therefore be likely to proceed at a slow pace, often during weekends and evenings. Motivation can often suffer because of this. Some schools will find it difficult to mobilise more than a handful of parents who are willing to give up their time. It is important to make sure that through their of lack of particular skills children are not used simply as 'slave labour'.

Vandalism

Vandalism can be a particular problem where school grounds are not secure at night and have unofficial access. Solutions to this problem may include the following:

- exclusion through improved boundary fencing and surveillance;
- participation by offenders in construction and planting improvements;
- vandal-proof structures and planting. This is difficult to achieve and may conflict with the need for a flexible, pleasant, detailed, child-scale environment.

Conflicts of interest

It may be that what teachers, lunchtime supervisors, school governors and parents want is in conflict with the desires of pupils. For example, it may be feared that increased vegetation will hinder supervision. Also some activities or features may conflict or be incompatible. Sensitive design should enable resolution of most conflicts.

Once you have considered these aspects it is time to get designing!

Stage 4   Creating designs

You have now to transform your goals and ideas into something concrete (not literally!).

Who designs?

It is very useful to be able to work with a landscape designer at this stage (see section on Who is going to help?). However, if this is not possible, teachers can work on design projects with children in the class. Or you may be able to employ an artist to work with pupils to develop some features or murals for the grounds. You may find it easiest for pupils to generate ideas for different parts of the grounds and to use staff to co-ordinate these into a whole. Or you may decide that it is not possible to involve pupils but you or a designer will interpret their ideas. We have tried to describe below some useful processes and ideas which you can develop with or without the aid of a landscape designer.

Designing

There are many ways of coming up with ideas for changing playgrounds. Design is a process where ideas are 'tossed about' and tested, usually through drawings, in the imaginative generation of alternative 'solutions'. The design process follows a course of gradual refinement towards these solutions. This all sounds daunting and perhaps a bit abstract, so below we have taken the 'structure' or anatomy of a typical school ground design apart and described its various parts in the hope that this gives you a picture of what makes up successful designs. Just as if we take apart an engine and study individual parts and their function we can learn how the whole engine fits together and works. It is important that the *whole* design be considered above its *parts* so that, for example, a pond is not constructed in one place and it is later discovered that it may have been better sited next to the nature area or within a school quad. Although we believe tackling the design of the grounds as a whole is most beneficial, if this seems too complex then start with one area or feature having carefully thought through siting in relation to other potential future developments.

Let's start with *what* you're designing with . . .

The raw materials of landscape design

The elements (e.g. landform) (see **Information Box 7.7**) and materials (e.g. timber) of landscape design can be thought of as being like the colours an artist uses: they are combined creatively by the designer to produce a 'whole environment' just as a painter creates a picture with colours on a canvas.

Designing is generating ideas for ways to use the elements of landscape design to achieve goals that have been set and overcome site problems.

What you need to design with

Designs can be worked out using pens, pencils or crayons on paper using a scaled base plan (see information-gathering stage) or through the use of scale models. You will no doubt be familiar with materials for model-making. Models have the obvious advantage of being three dimensional and therefore easier to understand than two-dimensional plans. But designing in plan has the advantage of speed and flexibility.

You can use all sorts of drawings and diagrams to illustrate ideas. You will eventually need to work to scale drawings unless you decide to construct or plant from schematic drawings. This is perfectly possible. Scale drawings get larger the more detail you need to show.

You may be lucky enough to have computers to generate designs.

Design sequence

Design is a process of gradual refinement. You begin by generating lots of alternative general ideas for spaces and activities (see below) which you select from and modify and eventually bring together into one scheme or plan for the whole school grounds.

INFORMATION BOX 7.7   ELEMENTS OF LANDSCAPE DESIGN

- Vegetation (trees, shrubs, climbing plants, grasses, herbaceous plants, bulbs, mosses)
- Hard surfacing
- Landform and level change
- Water
- Barriers (e.g. fences, walls)
- Furnishings (e.g. seats, lighting)
- Art and artefacts

You will then proceed to make detailed proposals for each part right through to choosing paint colours or plant species.

The anatomy of a school ground design

Below we study the 'parts' of a school ground design 'anatomy' (**Information Box 7.8**) and suggest ideas which we hope are useful to you when designing your grounds. We are guided by the need to reduce boredom, crowding, marginalisation, exclusion, playground aggression – the factors we identified as influencing bullying behaviour.

INFORMATION BOX 7.8   THE ANATOMY OF A SCHOOL GROUND DESIGN

- Zones and spaces
- Separating elements and edges
- Access, routes and trails
- Features
- Surfaces, finishes and furnishings

Zones and spaces

The first thing to consider when designing a school ground layout is the creation of spaces and zones.

Zones

Zones are areas that are used for similar or specific activities. They can be defined by these activities, e.g. active zone, passive or quiet zone, garden area, seating area. It should be possible to divide up the school ground site into a series of zones. Some of them will be based on existing patterns of use but most will be newly created.

It is useful to create zones as a way of defining the *primary* function of an area. Zoning solves the problem of existing conflicting uses which at present have to share one zone and enables you to ensure you are providing for a wide range of activities. **Information Box 7.9** lists some typical school ground zones.

INFORMATION BOX 7.9   SOME ZONES FOR THE SCHOOL
GROUNDS (DEFINED BY ACTIVITY)

- Garden area for cultivation
- Nature study area
- Active running and ball games area
- Quiet area
- Small games, loose equipment area
- Seating/eating area
- Adventure play area
- Outdoor work, hobby area
- Outdoor classroom or performance area
- Playground markings area
- Sand play area
- Water play area
- Ball play area
- Formal games area
- Fixed play structures area

Spaces

A space is a discrete or distinct place. A zone may be formed of several linked spaces or one space. Spaces can be described as 'outdoor rooms'. This analogy with indoor living environments is apt and useful. Spaces (and zones) should have 'walls' (e.g. planting, fences, lines on the floor, change of level) which separate them from other areas. They can (like a room in a house) be shaped, organised and furnished to create a physical and visual character appropriate to their function. Like the rooms in a house a space will have primary functions, e.g. sitting or adventurous play, but be flexible enough to be used for many different incidental purposes.

Illustrated in **Figure 7.4** is a sitting space with log seats within a school courtyard. It is small and intimate; 'an outdoor parlour', enclosed by planters, pool and the wall of the courtyard. It is located on the sunny side of the courtyard to take full advantage of the warmth here. This space can be used for reading, writing, small outdoor classes, sitting, talking and relaxing.

Locating and shaping spaces and zones

Deciding where spaces and zones will be is part of the site-planning process. This involves discussion of where the most suitable sites for activities are. To do this it is necessary to look at conflicts and problems as well as opportunities and to refer to your physical site survey.

Some examples of site opportunities are:

- an existing muddy grassed area with a few trees might form the basis for a nature or mini woodland area;
- an enclosed courtyard or quad with its restricted access and warm microclimate might be ideal for a teaching garden or for infants' water and sand play;
- ball games might be allocated to the end of an asphalt area where there is a high wall that balls can be bounced off.

Designing also means using landscape elements to overcome site specific problems. Examples of problem-solving are:

- *Problem* An existing garden is in a very shady site, rarely visited and badly neglected with few plants.

Figure 7.4 Sitting space with raised pond in school courtyard

Solution   The garden is relocated to sunny corner where the soil is better and the site is not being used for anything at present.

- *Problem*   A large area of tarmac is mainly used for football. The football keeps interfering with smaller children's games at one end.
  Solution   The football area is relocated to another playground. Or the football area is reduced in size and separate from the smaller children's area with planting and railway sleepers.

- *Problem*   The only existing seats in the playground are sited in the coldest, windiest spot and overlook a blank wall. No-one uses them much.
  Solution   Seats are moved and a seating area created elsewhere in sun or in dappled shade under trees with something, e.g. football, to look at.

Zones and spaces can be worked out by drawing circles or ovals on to the top of a base plan of the school grounds and discussing the suitability of each location and relationship of one zone to another. Alternatively this can be done using pieces of card each with a zone name written on it. These can be moved about on a base plan and 'pros and cons' of arrangements discussed. It is this sort of problem-solving that helps us plan the site successfully. Places are improved by making the most of what's there (opportunities) and making sure we change what has no potential (problems).

Shapes and size of spaces

It may be relatively easy to decide where spaces (and zones) should be but deciding what shape and size to make spaces is sometimes more difficult. Should they be circular, square, rectangular, oval, octagonal, hexagonal, semi-circular, kidney-shaped or amoeba-shaped?

The function of a space will often dictate its shape and size. For example, a football pitch will require a large rectangular area. A seating area may be small and semi-circular to create a 'snug' from which children can look out. Shapes that make awkward spaces are those which have acute internal angles: parallelograms, triangles, diamond/lozenge shapes.

Partial enclosure

Many spaces in the playground will be only partially enclosed by 'walls' or separating elements (see **Information Box 7.10**). Spaces can be open on one or two sides.

Semi-enclosed seating spaces have many advantages in playground designs. If attached to busy areas they can be used for onlooking, but provide shelter from the elements, balls and running children. They provide privacy and settings for social and imaginative games and yet can be easily supervised.

INFORMATION BOX 7.10   ELEMENTS THAT CAN BE USED TO
SEPARATE ZONES AND SPACES

- shrub planting and hedges
- planted boxes or tubs or tyres
- tyres
- benches
- ground modelling (mounding)
- changes of level
- fences, trellis or screens
- logs
- low brick, stone or railway sleeper walls

Separating elements and edges

You will have to make decisions on how the zones and spaces should be separated and
thus formed. What will the walls of your rooms be made of?

It is important to ensure that boundaries (separating elements) aren't too high.
Screens should be low enough to enable easy supervision and to prevent claustro-
phobic overpowering enclosures, but high enough to provide seclusion and shelter.
Information Box 7.10 lists some useful separating elements.

Designing positive edges to spaces

The way that edges (boundaries) of a space are designed can have a marked effect on
how well it functions. If successfully designed, edges are used by children as much if
not more than the centre of spaces.

Edges are good for sitting, onlooking, eating, resting, imaginative play, walking,
balancing, jumping, hiding. They should be designed for all of these activities.

Figures 7.5, 7.6 and 7.7 show a varied range of edges. The 'in and out' form of
the edges created with railway sleeper planters, seats, posts and planting increases the
surface area of the edge and thus 'absorbs' more children and their activities whilst
leaving large asphalted areas open for ball games and sports.

> **'The more nooks and crannies in the school grounds the
> better; for play, shelter and an improved playground
> microclimate.'**

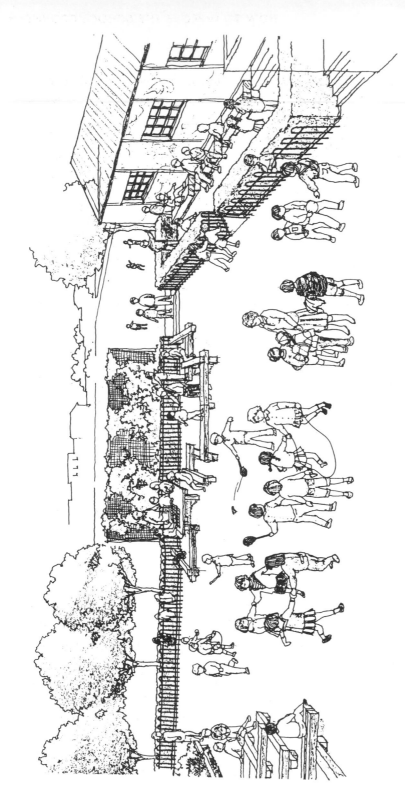

Figure 7.5 Perspective drawing showing use of new seating and planting

Access, routes and trails

The widest range of movement must be catered for but careful design should control and encourage different types of movement in different areas or restrict access where necessary.

Circulation in the playground should provide, first, for getting from 'A to B', e.g. from the school building to playground features or exit and, second, for play/recreational routes. A route can be designed to provide both or one of these functions. It is necessary to think about volumes of children that are expected in and between areas at different times of the day. Heavily used routes will need to be broad, smooth and hard paved. Occasional routes can be narrower with softer surfacing.

You can think in terms of a path hierarchy which is analogous to road classifications. In a school ground there will be, for pedestrians, the equivalent of 'Motorways', 'Major A roads', 'B roads' 'scenic routes' and 'rough tracks'.

Routes can be designed as a play experience. Examples of this type of route or trail are well illustrated in **Figures 7.8** and **7.9**. Trails can be made with painted shapes, or constructed of tyres, logs, stones. Trails can be used to connect different spaces or features.

Children also love 'secret routes' (and places). These can be provided whilst still enabling supervision through careful control of variation in height and nature of screening vegetation or fencing.

Vehicle and Service Access

It is important to ensure that access points for emergency and service vehicles are not blocked by new features in the design. Car parking should be segregated from play areas.

Features

A feature in the school ground design context can loosely be described as an element which attracts particular attention or is the focus for particular activities. Features can be designed for specific functions, e.g. balancing pole, or designed/selected for incidental or multi-functioning use, e.g. logs.

School grounds should contain as many varied features as possible to absorb children. This prevents a 'honey pot' situation where a few isolated features attract so much use that they deteriorate. This is a real danger when the first feature in a phased improvement of a school yard is constructed.

Features can be focal, e.g. climbing frame, seat, pond, mound, or linear, e.g. footprint or tyre trail, race track, nature trail, snake mound. They can be clustered e.g.

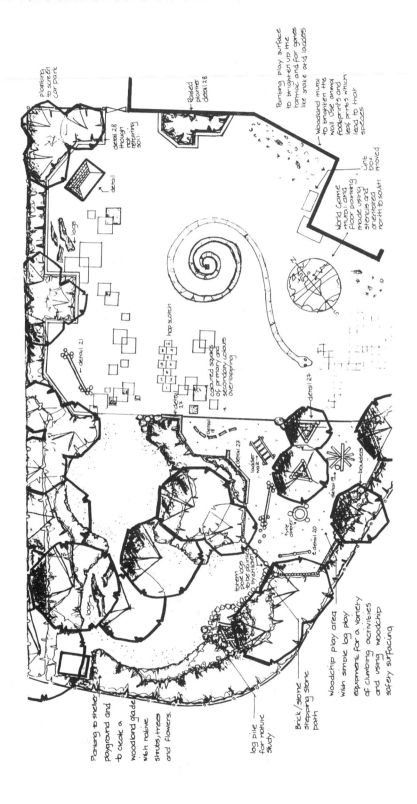

Figure 7.6 Plan of small school yard showing varied zones, spaces and edges

Figure 7.7 Edges can be diversified with railway planters and seats

in an adventure play area (**Figure 7.6**), or strung out like beads on a rosary forming incidents along trails.

For children many aspects of the environment become a focus of interest for different games and activities. As well as larger features, smaller incidental features (stones, handles, posts, textured surfaces) should also be retained or provided.

Changes of level, vantage points and water are features which are irresistible to children.

Artworks

Murals enliven the playground without taking up space. They provide colour and stimulation for the imagination and can incorporate games.

Children can and should be involved in all stages of designing and executing murals. They are quick to produce and can transform a bleak playground environment in a very short period. The floorscape is generally under-used for paintings.

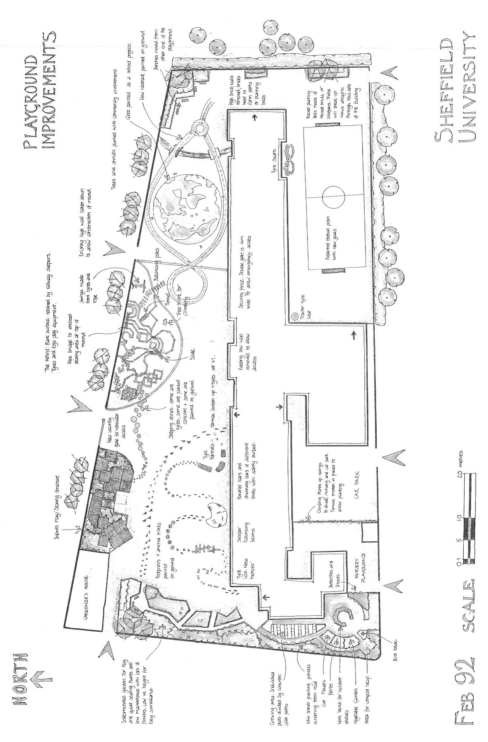

Figure 7.8 Plan of school ground design illustrating use of play trails

Figure 7.9 Stepping stones – timber, tyres and painted circles

Sculptures as well as providing visual stimulation can function as play, climbing, sitting or sound features. Temporary features or permanent sculptures can be constructed on a regular basis in an outdoor classroom or gallery area or in a nature area. Popular projects at present include environmental artworks such as woven willow structures or water-based works. Schools can work with artists on all of these projects.

Surfaces, finishes and furnishings

Once the design for the grounds has been worked out the nature of the materials that will be used and any decorative furnishings and finishes that are required should be decided. Equally, this can be decided during construction. It is important to consider the detail of texture, colour, tone and pattern of materials and plants. Some guidance is given below.

Surfaces

Ground surfacing materials are selected using practical, financial and aesthetic criteria. Practical issues often dictate choice of surfacing materials, and whether the surface is 'hard' (paved) or 'soft' (grass or low planting). Grass is unsuitable for heavily used areas as it soon becomes worn and muddy. Increasing the diversity of colour, texture and pattern in paving can help to transform the school ground. The floorscape can be a highly used and significant resource for children. The more complex and imaginative the floor the more opportunities there are for play. The use of coloured bitumen-based paints (although costly) is a great antidote to 'seas' of black asphalt. 'Murals' can be horizontal as well as vertical. Safety surfaces will be important under all climbing structures. Sand or bark are cheaper than matting but require more maintenance. Recycled materials will very often be available.

Finishes

Here finishes refers not only to coatings for, or texture of constructed elements but to the texture and colour of foliage or plants. As with the floorscape, diversity of colour, texture and pattern is the key to creating a satisfying environment for children. Detailed pattern or bright colours which may look fussy or garish to adults can be highly stimulating for children.

Furnishings

Furnishings means smaller elements or features (see above) which add to the comfort, enjoyment or ease of use of an environment. Like furnishings in a house they often have a decorative function. They include seating, lighting, handrails, litter bins and drinking fountains. It is particularly important that the scale of furnishings is appropriate for children, e.g. that the seats, handrails and litterbins are not too high.

Stage 5   Implementing the designs

In this part we give some guidance on implementation with some general points to consider. The way each school constructs and plants their playground will vary dramatically. The availability of materials, finance, technical expertise, voluntary and paid help will all influence the end result.

Sequence

It is desirable and usually necessary to phase implementation of your design. You may decide to carry out a project each year or each term. It is a good idea to start with a simple high impact project such as mural painting that rapidly transforms the environment. This can stimulate more interest in the school ground and further offers of help. You may also begin with small projects e.g. building one or two seats. These projects make a big difference but are relatively cheap and easy to construct. Once you have gained confidence and experience larger more complex projects can be tackled.

Labour and technical expertise

Voluntary labour as we have seen will probably form the backbone of the implementation of projects. This may include pupils, parents, staff and governors but also voluntary organisations such as conservation, community arts or play organisation volunteers. It is a good idea to check what help is available in your area. Don't forget that pupils should be involved whenever and however possible.

You may decide to pay for specialist services e.g. play equipment or safety surface installation. We advise that these are kept to a minimum for financial reasons but more importantly because the participation of the whole school community in the project plays a vital part in successfully influencing bullying behaviour. This can often be frustrating and a lack of technical expertise causes setbacks and reduced confidence. However, it is often the case that if enough people are involved, particularly parents, excellent skills are usually available.

Work day events can be organised, publicised in advance and achieve specific tasks.

Materials

It is on materials that most of your money will be spent. Recycled construction materials are very often used in schools projects. These can include railway sleepers, other second-hand timber (although be aware of hazardous preservatives, nails and other dangers) bricks, setts, broken paving slabs, logs, plastic pipes, tyres, broken pottery (for mosaics), bark.

Trees and shrubs can be raised from seed and cuttings by pupils – a good teaching exercise if you have time and space. Parents can often make plant donations, especially if they have a garden. Some organisations, such as the Tree Council, offer grants for tree planting. Inexpensive plants may be available from your local authority nursery.

Local suppliers may be able to offer materials at reduced rates or similarly make donations.

Tools and equipment

You will probably need to hire or borrow tools and equipment. Make sure you budget for this. A lot of work can be done with hand tools but you may need a small pneumatic drill for digging up tarmac.

Safety

Make sure you consult your local authority at the earliest possible stage in your project. Structures will have to meet specific criteria. Establish a safe practice code during construction and planting. Check on public liability insurance if you are involving parents and volunteers.

Ideas and examples

Ideas for construction and planting can be found in some of the books listed at the end of this chapter. You can also copy and adapt structures you have seen in other playgrounds, gardens or parks. You may gradually evolve structures on site using skills and know-how of volunteers.

Stage 6   Maintenance and review

Maintenance

It is extremely important that the maintenance of any improvements is considered before you begin designing and certainly before implementation. Plants will obviously require maintenance, especially grass. Weeding may need to be a frequent task although mulching can help to reduce this. Structures will need checking (for safety) and repairing. Fish need feeding. You can decide how much time is available for maintenance and try to design for this. It is essential that maintenance of the environment is built into the whole-school management system and, where possible, forms part of the curriculum. Weeding and litter collection can form part of everyday school activities using rotas and free time. This avoids the common problem of reliance on the work and commitment of one member of staff to keep areas maintained, and the deterioration of the environment once this person leaves the school. Local authority or private contractors will have to know how to manage new environments. Poor maintenance has been one of the most common problems for schools which have made changes, and has often led to complete failure of schemes, particulary ponds.

Codes of behaviour

It helps to set up codes of behaviour for different new structures or spaces. These codes can be set up by pupils themselves in discussion. This prevents misuse/vandalism, conflicts within, and therefore deterioration of areas. Sensitive environments or those that are specifically for educational purposes within the curriculum should have restricted access if necessary. The discussion and codes help with other anti-bullying strategies.

Monitoring improvements

You should be prepared to monitor the new environment and to adapt, repair and change structures and planting as necessary. It is useful to perceive the outdoor environment as a dynamic resource – making changes is the beginning of a process not an end result.

SUMMARY

We hope you find it possible to follow all or some of the process and ideas described above. The schools involved in our project which managed to change their grounds reported a marked reduction in the number of 'incidents' that had to be dealt with at the end of each play time. We hope that you find this too and that your improved environment, as well as helping to make bullying a thing of the past, provides many other future sources of pleasure and learning for staff and pupils alike.

E·I·G·H·T   # Resources

A bullying bibliography

This text provides a brief summary of all known published materials relating to bullying behaviour. It is about to be updated.

Skinner, A. (1992) *Bullying: an annotated bibliography of literature and resources.* Leicester: Youth Work Press.

Understanding bullying: background information

General texts and articles which provide information about the nature of the problem.

Besag, V. (1989) *Bullies and victims in schools.* Milton Keynes: Open University Press.

Bowers, L., Smith, P.K. and Binney, V. (1992) Cohesion and power in the families of children involved in bully/victim problems at school. *Journal of Family Therapy*, 14, 371–387.

DES (1989) *Discipline in schools: report of the commission chaired by Lord Elton.* London: HMSO.

Keise, C. (1992) *Sugar and spice: bullying in single sex schools.* Stoke on Trent: Trentham Books.

La Fontaine, J. (1991) *Bullying: a child's view*. London: Calouste Gulbenkian Foundation.

Nabuzoka, D., Whitney, I., Smith, P.K. and Thompson, D. (1993) Bullying and children with special educational needs in school. In D.P. Tattum (ed.) *Understanding and managing bullying*. London: Heinemann.

Smith, P.K. (1991) The silent nightmare: bullying and victimisation in school peer groups. *The Psychologist*, 4, 243–248.

Tattum, D.P. and Lane, D.A. eds. (1988) *Bullying in schools*. Stoke on Trent: Trentham Books.

Whitney, I. and Smith, P.K. (1993) A survey of the nature and extent of bullying in junior/middle and secondary schools. *Educational Research*, 35, 3–25.

Overviews of intervention strategies

The books in this section are edited books which contain a wide variety of chapters. These books will provide you with information about bullying and descriptions of different kinds of interventions.

Elliot, M. (ed.) (1991) *Bullying: a practical guide for schools*. London: Longman.

Roland, E. and Munthe, E. (eds) (1989) *Bullying: an international perspective*. London: David Fulton.

Smith, P.K. and Thompson, D. (eds) (1991) *Practical approaches to bullying*. London: David Fulton.

Smith, P.K. and Sharp, S. (eds) (1994) *School bullying: Insights and perspectives*. London: Routledge.

Tattum, D.P. (ed.) (1993) *Understanding and managing bullying*. London: Heinemann.

Establishing a whole-school anti-bullying policy

Packs, articles and texts which focus on whole-school approaches and policy development/ implementation.

Besag, V. (1992) *We don't have bullies here!* V. Besag, 57 Manor House Road, Jesmond, Newcastle-upon-Tyne NE2 2LY.

Foster, P. and Thompson, D. (1991) Bullying: towards a non-violent sanctions policy. In P. K. Smith and D. Thompson (eds) (1991) *Practical approaches to bullying*. London: David Fulton.

Islington Safer Cities Project (1990) *We can stop it!* London: Islington Safer Cities Project. Video and resource pack.

Johnstone, M., Munn, P. and Edwards, L. (1992) *Action against bullying: a support pack for schools*. The Scottish Council for Research in Education.

Scottish Council for Research in Education (1993) *Support schools against bullying: the second SCRE anti-bullying pack*. Scottish Council for Research in Education.

Tattum, D.P. and Herbert, G. (1990) *Bullying: a positive response*. Faculty of Education, South Glamorgan Institute of Higher Education, Cyncoed Road, Cardiff CF2 6XD.

Thompson, D. and Arora, T. (1991) Why do children bully? An evaluation of the long-term effectiveness of a whole-school policy to minimize bullying. *Pastoral Care in Education*, 9, 5–12.

Thompson, D. and Sharp, S. (1994) *Establishing whole-school policies on pastoral issues*. London: David Fulton.

Tackling bullying through the curriculum

Videos, books and packs for use in the classroom.

For adults

Brown, C., Barnfield, J. and Stone, M. (1990) *Spanner in the works: education for racial equality and social justice in white schools*. Stoke on Trent: Trentham Books.

Cowie, H. and Rudduck J. (1988) *Co-operative groupwork: an overview*. BP Educational Service, PO Box 30, Blacknest Road, Blacknest, Alton, Hampshire GU34 4NX. (Training guide and four practical volumes: 1. *Learning together, working together*; 2. *School and classroom studies*; 3. *Co-operative learning: traditions and transitions*; 4. *Co-operative groupwork in the multi-ethnic classroom*.)

Gobey, F. (1991) A practical approach through drama and workshops. In P. K. Smith and D. Thompson (eds.) *Practical approaches to bullying*. London: David Fulton.

Housden, C. (1991) The use of theatre workshop and role play in PSE in a secondary school. In P.K. Smith and D. Thomson (eds) *Practical approaches to bullying*. London: David Fulton.

Kreidler, W.J. (1984) *Creative conflict resolution: more than 200 activities for keeping peace in the classroom*. Glenview, Illinois: Goodyear Books.

McGrath, H. and Fancey, S. (1991) *Friendly kids, friendly classrooms: teaching social skills and confidence in the classroom*. Melbourne: Longman Cheshire.

Maines, B. and Robinson, G. (1991) *Stamp out bullying*. Bristol: Lame Duck Publishing. Video and handbook for staff.

Masheder, M. (1986) *Let's cooperate: activities and ideas for parents and teachers of young children for peaceful conflict solving*. London: Quaker Peace Education Project.

Meddis, W. (1992) The work and intentions of the Armadillo Theatre in Education Company. In H. Cowie (ed.) *Working directly with bullies and victims*. Conference Pack, Bretton Hall, W. Bretton, Wakefield, W. Yorks WF4 4LG.

NUT/City of Leicester Teachers' Association (1989) *Challenging oppression – lesbians and gays in school: a resources pack*. City of Leicester Teachers' Association.

SCCC (1992) *Speak-up: an anti bullying resource pack*. Scottish Consultative Committee on the Curriculum/South Edinburgh Crime Prevention Panel.

Shropshire County Council (1992) *Personal and social education and equal opportunities*. SECRU, Bourne House, Shrewsbury, Shropshire.

For older pupils

Atwood, M. (1990) *Cat's eye*. London: Virago.

Bowles, S. (ed) (1984) *A question of blood: stories of prejudice*. London: Collins Educational.

Casdagli, P. and Gobey, F. (1990) *Only Playing, Miss*. Stoke on Trent: Trentham Books/Professional Development Foundation. Script and drama ideas.

Central Independent Television (1990) *Sticks and Stones*. Video available from Community Unit, Central Television, Broad Street, Birmingham B1 2JP.

Coppard, Y. (1990) *Bully*. London: Bodley Head.

Cormier, R. (1988) *The chocolate war*. London: Armada.

Golding, W. (1954) *Lord of the flies*. London: Faber and Faber.

Greenwich Youth Action (1991) *We're here too!* Greenwich Youth Action, Plumcroft School, Genesta Road, London SE18 3PE. (Video which raises awareness about issues of disability.)

Guy, R. (1989) *The friends*. Harmondsworth: Penguin.

Hill, S. (1974) *I'm the king of the castle*. Harmondsworth: Penguin.

Lee, H. (1960) *To kill a mockingbird*. London: Heinemann.

Needle, J. (1979) *My mate Shofiq*. London: Armada Lyons.

Osler, A. (1989) *Speaking out: black girls in Britain*. London: Virago Upstarts.

Sallis, S. (1981) *Sweet Frannie*. Harmondsworth: Puffin Plus.

Swindells, R. (1988) *Brother in the land*. Harmondsworth: Penguin.

Taylor, M. (1990) *Roll of thunder, hear my cry*. Harmondsworth: Puffin.

Zindel, P. (1969) *The Pigman*. London: Bodley Head.

For younger pupils

Byars, B. (1992) *The eighteenth emergency*. London: Heinemann Education.

Central Independent Television (1990) *The trouble with Tom*. Video available from Community Unit, Central Television, Broad Street, Birmingham B1 2JP.

Chambers, A. (1991) *The present takers*. London: Mammoth.

Elliot, M. (1986) *Willow Street Kids*. London: Andre Deutsch.

Elliot, M. (1993) *The bullies meet the Willow Street kids*. London: Pan Macmillan Children's Books.

Godden, R. (1991) *The Diddakoi*. London: Pan.

Grunsell, A. (1989) *Bullying*. Gloucester: Gloucester Press.

Kemp, G. (1981) *Gowie Corby plays chicken*. Harmondsworth: Puffin.

Kumar, A. (1985) *The Heartstone Odyssey*. Allied Mouse. (The Heartstone Organisation can be contacted at Allied Mouse, First Floor, Longden Court, Spring Gardens, Buxton, Derbyshire SK17 68Z.)

Responding to bullying

Training materials and articles describing different approaches.

Arora, C.M.J. (1991) The use of victim support groups. In P. K. Smith and D. Thompson (eds) *Practical approaches to bullying*. London: David Fulton.

da Silva, C. and Ross, C. (1991) *I can look after myself!* London: Islington Education Authority.

Maines, B. and Robinson, G. (1992) *Michael's story: the no blame approach*. Bristol: Lame Duck Publishing. (Video and handbook.)

Penn Green Family Centre (1990) *Learning to be strong: developing assertiveness with young children*. Changing Perspectives Ltd., Riverside House, Winnington Street, Northwich, Cheshire CW8 1AD.

Pikas, A. (1989) The common concern method for the treatment of mobbing. In E. Roland and E. Munthe (eds) *Bullying: an international perspective*. London: David Fulton.

Lunchbreaks and playtimes

General texts, packs and training materials.

Adams, Eileen (1990) *Learning through landscapes team: a report on the design management and development of school grounds*. Winchester: Learning Through Landscapes Trust.

Birmingham City Council/National Primary Centre (1990) *Practice to share: the management of children's behavioural needs*. National Primary Centre, Westminster College, Oxford OX2 9AT.

Blatchford, Peter (1989) *Playtime in the primary school*. Windsor: NFER Nelson.

Blatchford, P. and Sharp, S. (eds) (1993) *Breaktime and the school: understanding and changing playground behaviour*. London: Routledge.

Boulton, M. and Smith, P.K. (1986) Rough and tumble play in children: environmental influences. *Playworld Journal*, 1, 15–17.

DES (1990) *The outdoor classroom: educational use, landscape design and management in school grounds*, Building Bulletin 71. London: HMSO

Imich, A. and Jefferies, K. (1989) Management of Lunchtime Behaviour. *Support for Learning*, 4, 46–52.

Karklins J. and Kirby, P. (1993) *Midday supervisors In-service programme: open learning pack*, Inspection Service and Training Services. Norfolk County Council, Norfolk Educational Press, County In-Service Centre, Witard Road., Norwich NR7 9XD.

Mares, C. and Stephenson, R. (1988) *Inside outside*. Brighton: Keep Britain Tidy Group Schools Research Project.

OPTIS, (1986) *Lunchtime Supervision*. Oxfordshire Programme for Training, Oxfordshire County Council.

Robinson, M. and Weston, N. (1990) *Primary lunchtime resource pack*. Education Support Service, Silverhill Centre, Stocksfield Avenue, Newcastle upon Tyne.

Ross, Carol and Ryan, Amanda (1990) *Can I stay in today, Miss? – Improving the school playground*. Stoke on Trent: Trentham Books.

Sharp, S. and Smith, P.K. (1993) Making changes to playtime. *Topic*. Windsor: NFER.

Sharp, S., Sellars, A. and Cowie, H. (1994) Time to listen: setting up a peer counselling service to tackle bullying. *Pastoral Care in Education*.

Sheat, Lyndal (1991) *Why improve our school grounds?* School Grounds Design Pack, Department of Landscape, Sheffield University.

Yorkshire and Humberside Chapter (1981) *Schoolyard Landscape*. London: The Landscape Institute.

Governors

Advisory Centre for Education (1990) Governors and bullying. *ACE Bulletin*, 34.

Families

Besag, V. (1991) Parents and teachers working together. In M. Elliot (ed.) *Bullying: a practical guide for schools*. London: Longman.

Kidscape (1990) *Keep them safe*. London: Kidscape.

Mellor, A. (1993) *Bullying and how to fight it: a guide for families*. Scottish Council for Research in Education.

Pearce, J. (1989) *Fighting, teasing and bullying: simple and effective ways to help your child*. Wellingborough: Thorsons.

Helpful organisations

Anti-Bullying Campaign, 10 Borough High Street, London SE11 9QQ. Tel.: 071 378 1446.

British Trust for Conservation Volunteers, 36 St. Mary's Street, Wallingford, Oxfordshire OX10 OEU. (For information and volunteers for nature conservation work.)

Childline, Second Floor, Royal Mail Building, Studd Street, London N1 OQJ. Tel.: 071 239 1000.

Kidscape, 152 Buckingham Palace Road, London SW1W 9TR. Tel.: 071 730 3300.

The Landscape Institute, 6/7 Barnard Mews, London SW11 1QU. (For advice on landscape designers and their appointment.)

Learning through Landscapes, Third Floor, Southside Offices, The Law Courts, Winchester, Hants SO23 9DL. Tel.: 0962 846258. (Information on improving school grounds for education, newsletter and membership.)

National Association for Pastoral Care in Education, NAPCE Base, c/o Education Dept., University of Warwick, Coventry CV4 7AL. Tel.: 0203 523 810.

Tree Council, 35 Belgrave Square, London SW1X 8QN. (For grant aid for tree planting.)

Index